Words Into Worlds:
Learning a Second Language
Through Process Drama

CONTEMPORARY STUDIES IN SECOND LANGUAGE LEARNING

A Monograph Series Dedicated to Studies in Acquisition and Principled Language Instruction

Robert J. Di Pietro, editor

The Catalan Immersion Program: A European Point of View
Josep Maria Artigal

A Developmental Psycholinguistic Approach to Second Language Teaching
Traute Taeschner

Reading Development in a Second Language: Theoretical, Empirical, and Classroom Perspectives
Elizabeth B. Bernhardt

Vygotskian Approaches to Second Language Research
James P. Lantolf and Gabriela Appel, editors

Bilingualism and Testing: A Special Case of Bias
Guadalupe Valdes and Richard Figueroa

Elizabeth B. Bernhardt, editor

Listen to the Silences: Mexican American Interaction in the Composition Classroom and Community
Kay Losey

Input Processing and Grammar Instruction in Second Language Acquisition
Bill VanPatten

Words Into Worlds: Learning a Second Language Through Process Drama
Shin-Mei Kao and Cecily O'Neill

Words Into Worlds:
Learning a Second Language
Through Process Drama

by

Shin-Mei Kao
National Cheng Kung University

and

Cecily O'Neill
Ohio State University

Ablex Publishing Corporation
Stamford, Connecticut
London, England

Printed in the United States of America

Library of Congress Cataloging-in-Publication Data

Kao, Shin-Mei
    Words into worlds : learning a second language through process drama / by Shin-Mei Kao and Cecily O'Neill.
        p. cm.—(Contemporary studies in second language learning)
    Includes bibliographical references and index.
    ISBN 1-56750-368-3 (cloth).— ISBN 1-56750-369-1 (paper)
    1. Language and languages—Study and teaching. 2. Drama in education. I. O'Neill, Cecily. II. Title. III. Series.
    P53.297.K36 1998
    418'.007–DC21   97-41886
                                                CIP

Ablex Publishing Corporation   Published in the U.K. and Europe by:
100 Prospect Street   JAI Press Ltd.
Stamford, CT 06901   38 Tavistock Street
                                       Covent Garden
                                       London WC2E 7PB
                                       England

P

Contents

Preface

Language teachers nowadays have available a wide range of drama activities for engaging students' participation and promoting active learning in the classroom. These include language games, storytelling, role-play, simulations, scenarios, prepared and spontaneous improvisation, and process-oriented drama activities. In addition to these "informal" drama approaches, there is also the more formal and traditional method in which participants study a scene or play and then perform it in front of an audience, as in theatre. The difference between these two approaches is that, as Dorothy Heathcote, the British drama educator, points out, "The difference between the theatre and the classroom is that in the theatre everything is contrived so that the audience gets the kicks. In the classroom the participants get the kicks" (in Johnson & O'Neill, 1984, p. 158). The distinction between formal theatre and informal drama activities in educational settings was clarified in the 1950s and '60s when Peter Slade and Brian Way emphasized the developmental aspects of drama. They believed that drama activities could be used to increase individual awareness, self-expression, and creativity. Later, Dorothy Heatcote, Gavin Bolton, and other drama educators shifted the focus from using drama for personal development to an emphasis on the significance of drama in the learning process. They stressed the importance of understanding how drama activities can be designed and structured in the classroom in order to promote insights into subject matter, motivate research and the pursuit of knowledge, and facilitate the development of language. Their concern with content and the broader functions of drama has led to its increasing acceptance as an educational tool as well as a separate subject in the curriculum.

The approach advocated by Heathcote and Bolton is known as "drama in education" or "educational drama." In the early '90s, a new term, "process drama," emerged among drama educators in the United States and

Australia. This refers to drama activities that aim to go beyond short-term, teacher-dominated exercises. Instead, the drama is extended over time and is built up from the ideas, negotiations, and responses of all the participants in order to foster social, intellectual, and linguistic development. Although a process-oriented approach is increasingly familiar to educators in various first language settings, it is still new to many second language teachers. Consequently, there is little related literature dealing with underlying theory, the evaluation of its outcomes and practical guidelines for using it for the different purposes of second language teaching and learning.

As drama and language teachers, we feel that this approach is fundamentally different in its functions and outcomes from other more familiar drama techniques. This experiential intuition led us to try out process drama in various ESL, EFL, and immersion classrooms with different levels, backgrounds, and ages of learners in order to teach subject matter, literature, basic conversation, reading, writing, and so forth. Our classroom experience encouraged us to look further into what actually takes place when drama is used during the learning process. Borrowing Heathcote's term, we were interested in how drama "kicks" the participants, how participants react to these kicks, and how to develop drama that delivers kicks effectively! This book is a record of our investigations.

The book is divided into three parts. The first part lays the theoretical groundwork for using process drama in second language teaching and learning. In Chapter One, we briefly introduce the characteristics of a range of different drama activities and propose that all drama approaches can be arranged along a continuum with "closed" communication at one end and "open" communication at the other, depending on the discourse generated, the roles involved, the tasks promoted, and the functions achieved. Chapter Two provides a detailed discussion of some of the critical aspects of conducting effective drama activities. These include starting the drama, choosing appropriate themes, defining the roles of the teacher and the learners, evoking dramatic tension, promoting engagement, the function of non-verbal participation, reflection, and the relationship of the drama experience to real life. These various aspects are illustrated by actual drama activities from our own classrooms.

The second part of the book considers some empirical studies of the effects and outcomes of drama activities used to promote open communication. Chapter Four focuses on the nature of the discourse and interactions produced by different drama activities. Chapter Five discusses the participants' response to process drama from a socio-psychological perspective. Our intention is to draw the attention of language educators using drama to the importance of systematically investigating how drama actually works in real settings. Enthusiastic language teachers have long insisted on the usefulness of drama activities, but their claims have been based solely on their intuition and experience and have been disputed for this reason. We hope that this part of the book will inspire teachers to undertake more classroom studies of different aspects of drama in language teaching and learning. This will lead to a better understanding of these approaches and will help to improve the quality of second language education.

The third section of the book moves to more practical matters: planning a drama-oriented course and evaluating the outcomes of teaching and learning. Chapter Five proposes a model that should help teachers to develop a drama curriculum based on a consideration of educational policy, approach, syllabus, materials, learners, and the classroom. Chapter Six discusses several evaluation procedures for gathering different kinds of data in a drama course. We suggest that there is no single assessment that will provide a complete picture of what the learners have achieved. Therefore evaluating the learners and the course from different angles will be necessary.

We started preparing this book in 1992. It is difficult to express in words how much we appreciate all the support and help we have received in the past few years from our colleagues, families, friends, and students. We feel especial gratitude to the general editor of this series, Dr. Elizabeth Bernhardt, who inspired us with the idea of writing this book and provided continuous encouragement and comment. Many thanks go to our colleagues and students at Ohio State University, USA, and National Cheng Kung University, Taiwan, who participated enthusiastically in the projects that led to this book. We also appreciate the National Science Council of the Republic of China for its financial support of the studies presented in chapters Three and Four. Finally, we thank Dr. Ferenc Pinter as a colleague and an honest friend for developing a computer model to score the data in our studies and for his valuable comments on the manuscript.

Shin-Mei Kao
Cecily O'Neill

1

A Continuum of Drama Approaches in Second Language Learning and Teaching

INTRODUCTION

S econd language teachers have long been familiar with the use of different dramatic activities to create opportunities for a variety of classroom interactions in the target language. Drama strategies available in the second language classroom range from exercise-based games, short rehearsed scenes presented in the classroom, brief role-plays, planned simulations, scenarios, to the more challenging and extended mode of "process drama," the approach we present in this book. The usefulness of every kind of drama in second language (L2) teaching lies in the fact that it provides contexts for multiple language encounters and encourages authentic dialogue between teachers and students. As a result, the usual classroom interactions are profoundly and productively altered.

An increased emphasis on language use as well as on language knowledge is recognized as a priority among L2 teachers (Deckert, 1987). Research findings document the value of drama in the development of competence and confidence in using the target language. Positive attitudes to learning and an increase in social and cognitive skills among students have also been noted. The use of drama approaches make unique demands on the teacher, who will be required to assume functions in these activities that go beyond the more usual ones of an instructor, model and resource. It is obvious that the flexibility and inventiveness of the teacher is paramount in effective language teaching. These qualities will, consequently, inspire confidence and linguistic skills among students. Through drama, teacher and students together enter the world of increasingly authentic scenarios and creative dialogues.

DIALOGUE AND DRAMA

Dialogue is inherent in any form of dramatic event, however brief, fragmentary or informal it may be. It is the framework on which most drama and all speech is constructed. Di Pietro (1983) noted that the dramatic element in language is difficult to define, but acknowledged that its presence in dialogue enhances learning. In fact, dialogue is essential to every kind of language learning and as Bahktin (1986) points it out, dialogue is the simplest and most classic form of oral communication. Since the time of Socrates dialogue has been known as an ideal vehicle for delivering instruction. A classroom based on dialogue demands what Friere (1972) has called a horizontal relationship between participants. This horizontal relationship is the logical consequence of mutual trust between the participants and mutual trust happens to be one key element for drama participants to create meaningful dialogue in improvised scenes. Therefore, drama is likely to promote the horizontal relationship that Friere has suggested, so as to bring changes in the patterns of classroom communication and interaction. The significance these changes make in L2 education is the central theme of this book.

Drama gives students the vicarious experience of a variety of situations, attitudes, roles and worlds. When students are involved in creating and maintaining dialogues in fictional dramatic situations—the primary purpose of drama—a range of significant learnings occur. For example, in order to move the action forward, students need to activate their language knowledge so that their meaning can get through. Since the dramatic situations are under the control of the entire group and not the teacher alone, students develop a kind of ownership toward the activity. Therefore each student is intrinsically involved in developing dialogue so that the social interaction of the drama may continue. With the unique verbal contribution of each participant, the scope and depth of the activity is extended and every participant benefits from the drama experience.

THE DEVELOPMENT OF DRAMA IN EDUCATION

Drama in education puts an emphasis on the immediacy and informality of improvised activities rather than on the quality of performance. It originates from children's play and its justification comes from the principles of child-centered Progressive Education. Winifred Ward of Northwestern University established Creative Dramatics as an important part of the education of children and of teachers who teach children in the twenties and thirties. There were similar developments in Britain during the 1940s and 1950s, when spontaneity, creativity, self-expression, and personal growth were the goals of drama in education, rather than formal presentations and the acquisition of theater skills and knowledge. In recent years, the goals of social skills and personal growth dominant in the 1960s and early 1970s have given way to an understanding of drama as an essentially cognitive, social, and aesthetic process concerned with the negotiation of meaning.

The opportunities for active involvement in learning offered by the methodology of drama are exploited in all aspects of the curriculum in the first language setting. Subjects such as language art, social studies, history, and literature, incorporate drama techniques to achieve specific curriculum aims because drama is powerful for the kind of learning which does not merely concern personal growth but engages with significant moral, social, and political issues. For instance, drama has been used successfully to help students understand an event in history or elaborate a character or situation in literature; drama is also useful in developing and exercising social or linguistic skills. This increased seriousness has largely replaced the rather aimless games and improvisations that characterized some drama approaches in the 1970s. The success of these particular strategies may be judged by the extent to which the educational objectives are achieved. Wagner (1988) offers a summary of research, documenting the significance of drama in education in the development of oral language, literacy, motivation, positive attitudes, and social and cognitive skills.

DRAMA AND SECOND LANGUAGE LEARNING

The use of drama strategies in L2 teaching has closely paralleled the growth of drama in education. Some teachers feel able to offer students the opportunity to encounter language through drama in purposeful and challenging contexts, but there is no doubt that in many classrooms the work remains exercise-based, short-term, and teacher-controlled. As a result, the potential for learning is diminished.

Research suggests that while language teachers accept in principle that drama activities can help them achieve their goals, a disappointingly large number seem to restrict their efforts to the simplest and least motivating and enriching approaches, such as asking students to recite prepared scripts for role-play. The emphasis has tended to be on the accuracy of the language that is being used rather than on the meaning that is being conveyed. Di Pietro (1983) suggested that exercises designed to convey infor-mation—for example about the weather or a trip to France—occupy most of the attention of language teachers. Such exercises are unlikely to lead to mastery of the target language, since the motor that propels language acquisition is the desire to do things with words (Austin, 1962).

Drama does things with words. It introduces language as an essential and authentic method of communication. Drama sustains interactions between students with the target language, creating a world of social roles and relations in which the learner is an active participant. Drama focuses on the negotiation of meaning (Snyman & De Kock, 1991). The language that arises is fluent, purposeful and generative because it is embedded in context. Students are required by this context to be alert, to listen, and to demonstrate their understanding in immediate and imaginative responses. By helping to build the drama context, they develop their social and lin-guistic competence as well as listening and speaking skills. They grow in the capacity to engage in increasingly complex and creative communica-tive situations.

In a typical classroom, the role of the teacher determines learner activ-ity, based on the assumption that learners can only learn from their appointed instructors, but not from each other. As Widdowson (1990) makes clear, this kind of pedagogy fails to exploit the collective potential of learners as a resource for learning. In contrast, drama temporarily sus-pends the classroom context in favor of new contexts, new roles and new relationships. These make very different language demands on both teach-ers and students, so new possibilities of language use and development are opened up. One of the important features of the shift to the "as if" context of drama is that it has the potential to change quite significantly the pat-terns of communication and interaction in a classroom, and the teacher's part in those patterns (Byron, 1986).

Acts of identification and impersonation, that is, role-taking and role-creating, are at the core of all dramatic activity, whatever informal and improvised it may be. But, as Courtney (1992) points out, when students take on these identifications and impersonations they also engage cogni-tively with the other person. The more challenging the imagined situation, the more demands will be made on the participants to engage in the drama. Brief language exercises do little more than drill students for pre-dictable responses. Process drama, on the other hand, provides a signifi-cant context in which roles and identifications become detailed and complex. It elicits a variety of language registers corresponding to the dra-matic circumstances. Language acquisition arises from the urge to do things with words, and this need becomes paramount in process drama, when participants are required to manipulate the dramatic circumstances to achieve their own goals.

A CONTINUUM OF DRAMA APPROACHES

It is possible to arrange the spectrum of available drama approaches in a continuum from totally controlled language exercises and scripted role-plays through the semi-controlled approach of the scenario, to the kind of open communication of process drama. Figure 1.1 shows the relative positions of various drama approaches that are frequently used in various L2 classrooms. These are organized on a continuum according to the teaching and learning perspectives they offer.

Closed and Controlled Drama Approaches

L2 teachers appear to prefer to use *language games* and *simple scripted or rehearsed role-plays* which represent the most controlled and closed perspective on language learning. Language games are exercised-based competitions which often require participants to use some pre-determined sentence patterns or structures to complete some tasks. For example, a game called "The seat on my left is free" aims to get the students accustomed to using each other's names. To play it, the students sit in a circle with one chair left empty. The person with an empty seat on the left says: "The seat on my left is free, and I'd like so-and-so to sit next to me." The person whose name is called should move to the empty chair, leaving his/her own chair vacant. The person who has the empty seat on the left repeats the process till the organizer calls a halt (Maley & Duff, 1991, pp. 70–71). In this game, the students will get familiar with the sentence structure: "I'd like so-and-so to sit next to me," and will also practice the pronunciation of each other's name.

Scripted or rehearsed role playing is a kind of informal performance with no audience, costumes and props. Participants take pre-determined roles and play within the confines of previously determined "rules" or scenarios. Many L2 course books focusing on spoken skills use this technique to demonstrate how to achieve certain goals with particular sentence patterns. For example, to teach learners how to send a letter in the post office, the lesson usually contains a dialogue between the clerk and the customer about buying stamps, addressing envelopes, mailing procedures, and so on. After the teacher explains the context (e.g., the customs of doing business in the post office of the target culture), particular sentence structures (e.g., "Can I send this letter to Canada?," "How long will it take for the letter to get there?"), and related vocabulary (e.g., "postage," "air mail," "express mail," "mail box,") the learners are usually asked to practice the given dialogue in pairs and later to play the two roles in front of the class. This type of role-play allows the learners to internalize the desired linguis-

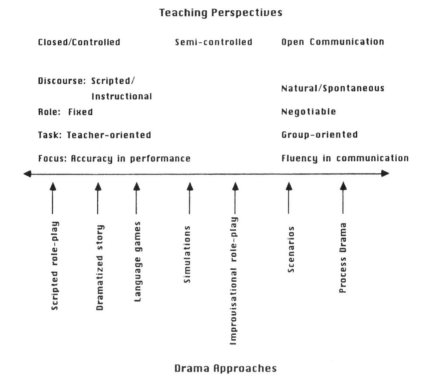

FIGURE 1.1. **A continuum of different drama approaches for L2 teaching and learning**

tic patterns after repeated practices. The learners are expected to use accurately what they have role-played in real situations.

These techniques may be designed to encourage students to perform particular linguistic structures, practice particular idioms, or recite lines according to pre-written scripts using certain items of vocabulary. The problem is that these experiences lack any resemblance to authentic language interactions. A minimum of context is supplied for such exercises, and they contain little that is unexpected or unpredictable. Because of repeated rehearsal and the simplicity of the interactions involved, these tasks may at first appear to produce language that is fluent and accurate. However, retention and transfer of learning may be disappointing, since no self-generated communication is taking place during these activities.

Short dramatic performances also find their place at this end of the spectrum. Many of the practical guides for L2 teachers about the use of classroom plays argue that students engaging in these activities increase their linguistic and socio-linguistic competence. Students who undertake this kind of pre-scripted drama will discover that it bears little relationship to the kind of verbal interactions that occur in the real world. The challenge for the students in this method lies in the demands of presentation rather than in any struggle for communication.

Simulations and simple role-plays can be equally prescriptive and limiting. They are activities that provide participants with opportunities to practice taking on pre-determined roles with particular attitudes and values in straightforward social situations. The situations are selected in order to introduce specific items of vocabulary, practice particular structures or reinforce previous learning. There is no pre-written script; instead, the participants are given detailed description of the roles they will play plus some situation cards setting the tasks they are going to fulfill. The most basic kind of role-play or simulation may not involve students in adopting a role other than their own; the situation in which they are placed is usually realistic in terms of the culture of the target language, for example, a visit to the baker's or the purchase of items of food at the local market. Similar cross-cultural training simulations are often used to prepare business men, government employees, and academic professionals for life in foreign cultures.

The problem of this method lies in the limitation of the number of situations the course designer can anticipate and provide for the participants. In other words, no matter how realistic the situation appears to be, something unexpected might happen in the scene in real life. Exercises in this category will probably focus initially on accuracy, the transmission of information, and growing familiarity with simple social interactions. Students may be asked to undertake brief exercises like these:

1. You visit the store to make some purchases. Inquire about the cost of several items.
2. Make an apology to a passer-by whose packages you have accidentally knocked to the ground.

Yet to the teacher who has the confidence to try, even these simple beginnings offer the possibility of enlarging the context and building on its interactive possibilities in order to generate a more dynamic encounter, both socially and linguistically. Using the second example above with students working in pairs, the roles could be expanded and the interactive quality of the exercise enhanced as follows:

Role A: You are trying to catch a bus and you inadvertently run into a passer-by loaded with packages. What will you say to this person? Remember the bus is about to leave.

Role B: You have just bought some delicate china, and someone has bumped into you, knocking your packages to the ground. What will you say to this person?

In this role-play there is a context and some degree of tension, but it is clear that both roles and language registers are still strictly limited by the confines of the exercise.

It is a simple matter for the teacher to set up useful exercises of this kind. Typically, they require students to use a variety of different functions of language: informing, describing, re-telling, persuading, questioning, and so on. Such activities may easily be made more challenging and more authentic by asking students to take on simple fictional roles. The fact that they will be adopting attitudes and qualities rather different from their own allows a degree of distance and releases them to some extent from a concern with the accuracy of their performance. For example, one student might adopt the role of an old lady who has lost her purse. She tries to explain to her partner, who has taken on the role of a police officer, exactly what has happened. Even such a simple interaction is likely to challenge the students' language resources, especially if the levels of the fictional roles are enhanced, by, for example, suggesting that the old lady is hysterical, deaf, or bewildered, and that the police officer is preoccupied with other duties. The move towards fictional roles and situations, we believe, correlates with increased fluency and confidence.

This kind of activity requires students to operate with at least a tacit understanding of the other person's point of view. As a result, they are given some opportunity to grow in fluency in a very protected situation. There is little tension and almost no interpretation or negotiation required within the situation, however, since roles and attitudes are known in advance and tasks are clearly set. The usual kind of dialogues practiced by students are likely to remain semantically impoverished, and roles are limited and stereo-typed. However, within these limits, success in maintaining the verbal interaction is almost always an outcome for the students.

It is possible to isolate key aspects of activities like these, which occur at the controlled and closed communication end of the continuum of drama approaches (also see Figure 1.2). These aspects include objectives, organization, context, roles, tension, decisions, and teacher function. For the kind of exercise described above, they may be summarized as follows:

The *objectives* of these exercises are to increase the learners' linguistic accuracy and to maintain a certain level of interaction during the activities, which are usually carried out in the form of *pair-work, small-group work*, and *rehearsal* in simple and naturalistic *contexts* selected by the teacher. The *roles* have fixed attitudes and are also determined by the teacher. Few *decisions* are made by the participants. The *tension* of the exercise arises because of the need for students to produce accurate language and vocabulary. The *functions* of the teacher are to set up the exercises, provide a resource for the students and eventually evaluate their efforts. These closed and controlled drama techniques are useful for learners at the beginning level when they do not possess sufficient knowledge about the target language to deal with uncertainty. However, the pre-determined features of these activities restrict learners from progressing to higher levels in using the target language.

Semi-Controlled Drama Approaches—Scenarios

Moving from the closed end of the continuum toward increasingly open communication, more innovative drama approaches include improvised role-plays and scenarios, reflecting a semi-controlled teaching perspective. These approaches offer social and linguistic environments in which learners interact with each other with greater authenticity. The scenario, or Strategic Interaction (SI)—an approach to language teaching developed by Robert Di Pietro, is one of the more elaborate methods (Di Pietro, 1987a). Di Pietro defines a scenario as "a thematically cohesive event in which humans perform actions that are purposeful to each of them." It comes closest to process drama in its structure and in its emphasis on tension and authenticity. Di Pietro's notion of Strategic Interaction goes beyond the short-term, task-oriented, teacher-dominated exercises described earlier, and is more closely aligned structurally with the ways in which drama activities have been used in other areas of education.

In the SI approach, the language classroom where students endlessly practice out-of-context dialogues is recognized as artificial and largely ineffectual. Instead, each lesson is divided into three phases: rehearsal, performance, and de-briefing. The technique stresses fluency over accuracy, while comprehension is the main aim. This process is quite different in both its aims and its outcomes from the kind of "performance" required when prepared scripts are memorized and presented. SI establish situations that contain genuine challenges, and require students to comprehend the cultural and social attitudes on which these situations are based.

The SI is a thematically cohesive and purposeful event in which students create their own dialogue and make decisions as to outcomes. Each scenario will have at least two interacting roles, and each role will have vested interests or attitudes that intersect with those of the opposing role. The students have to respond in their own way to the challenge of communication contained in the interaction. Their attention is shifted from language as an artifact to be mastered to a communicative goal to be reached. Dorothy Heathcote, the British drama educator, echoes this emphasis in her belief that effective drama is achieved by taking students' minds off themselves and focusing it outward on the tasks or challenge presented to them in the drama (in Johnson & O'Neill, 1984). The following is an example of a complex scenario theme proposed by Di Pietro:

> You are an American student attending to a university in Italy. You receive two invitations for the evening. One is from a professor who has asked you to dinner and wishes to discuss a research project you are eager to undertake. This professor is not an easy person to become familiar with and such an invitation is truly exceptional. The other invitation is from a student organization which offers considerable discounts for living expenses in their modern apartments. You do not have much money and you need to find less expensive quarters. This invitation will be the only one that the student organization will give out for the year. If you don't go, you may not be put on the favored list for an apartment. (Di Pietro, 1982a, p. 3)

In responding to this challenging situation, students are free to decide with whom they wish to interact, and what strategies they will chose. Groups of students are assigned a single role to fulfill, and, working together, they come to a decision. Some may volunteer to represent the role, while others contribute to the discussion and the decision. They try to anticipate the reaction of the other roles and time is given for some rehearsal of these possible interactions before the situation is played out. The rehearsal and informal performance may be audio- or video-recorded. In the final phase of the lesson, the teacher leads a de-briefing session in which difficult or inappropriate linguistic and interactional elements are discussed. For a follow-up activity, the students refine the preliminary dialogue they created during the first two phases based on the recorded data and the comments obtained in the de-briefing session. They can also formally perform the scene later according to their refined script.

Scenarios are always composed of people in a particular relation to each other, achieving goals that are motivating, linguistically challenging and culturally and personally meaningful. The emphasis is on reaching a communicative goal within the shelter of the group, in other words, through group participation in sense-making. This personal and social involvement is central to the success of the method, as Di Pietro recognized. Students care more about a situation and the information it contains, and understand it better when they have worked to make its meaning (Tannen, 1989).

Di Pietro clearly understood that to set up this kind of communication environment makes considerable demands on the flexibility and skills of the teacher. He proposed that the teacher's functions should go far beyond that of instructor and should include those of guide, counselor, consultant, coach, observer, evaluator, commentator, and discussion leader. Although the students have a certain degree of autonomy in deciding how to respond within the scenario, the teacher is very much responsible for the design of the activities and their progress.

Central differences between this approach and earlier efforts requires a fundamental change of stance by the teacher, including an understanding of the structural and dynamic qualities of every dramatic encounter and a recognition that language learning is both a personal and a social endeavor. For Di Pietro, the essential elements of Strategic Interaction include

1. the ability of language to create and engage students in new roles, situations and worlds;
2. dynamic tension;
3. the motivating and challenging power of the unexpected;
4. the tactical quality of language acquired under the stress of achieving a goal;
5. the linguistic and psychological ambiguity of human interaction;
6. the group nature of the enterprise; and
7. the significance of context.

All these aspects of SI are also key characteristics of process drama. The single element that immediately marks out Di Pietro's approach from more limited language exercises is his understanding of the significance of *tension* as the key element in dramatic dialogue, and, by extension, in every kind of significant language interaction.

Di Pietro understood that traditional classroom role-play offers little real choice to students. He recognized that motivation comes from the opportunity to take on diverse roles in situations that are as authentic and dynamic as possible. In a true dramatic interaction, there is a need to determine, interpret, and respond to the kinds of role being played by others and to cope with any potential interactional ambiguity. This ambiguity is a perfect reinforcement of the need to listen. In Strategic Interaction, in spite of role intentions and deliberations during the rehearsal phase, outcomes remain unpredictable. Validating the students' own themes and ideas is fundamental to this way of working, and gives them a measure of control over the content of the circumstances as well as a sense of empowerment. SI promotes a feeling of control that is not possible with closed role-plays and memorized dialogues, and this growing competence and ownership can be genuinely uplifting (Di Pietro, 1982b). SI encourages a sense of community and challenges the students to communicate. The key aspects of this approach may be summarized as follows:

The *objectives* of SI and simple improvisations are to increase the fluency and authenticity of the students' speech and their confidence in speaking.

The activities are partly rehearsed in *small groups* but retain a degree of unpredictability. At the initial stage, the *contexts* are partly determined by the teacher and further developed by the students in consultation with the teacher as the activity moves forward. Students may function as *group members, spokespersons* for the group, or may take on *individual roles* in the activity. *Decisions* are determined by the students' responses. The *teacher* functions as an initiator, challenger and resource provider. The *tension* arises from the social dynamic rather than from a focus on linguistic accuracy.

Open Communication—Process Drama

In Britain, and increasingly in the United States, drama in education has been refined and developed as both a powerful medium for learning and an art process in its own right. A fairly recent development in the field is known as "process drama." This term emerged in the United States and Australia in 1990, to distinguish this complex approach from more limited improvisations, skits, dramatized stories and creative dramatics. This term also helped to clarify the difference between this approach and those which emphasize performance (O'Neill, 1995). In Britain the terms "educational drama" and "drama in education" are almost synonymous with process drama.

Unlike brief improvisation exercises, process drama is concerned with the development of a wider context for exploration—a dramatic world created by the teacher and students working together within the experience. The key characteristics of process drama include active identification with and exploration of fictional roles and situations by the group. The aims of the work are to develop students' insight and to help them understand themselves and the world in which they live. This understanding is achieved through the exploration of significant dramatic contexts, and the outcomes do not necessarily include any kind of performance or presentation (O'Neill & Lambert, 1982). The "end product" of process drama is always the experience itself and the reflection that it can generate. Dorothy Heathcote, the drama educator who is most closely associated with these developments, believes that drama is never merely stories retold in action but situations confronting and changing human beings (Johnson & O'Neill, 1984). These situations involve people in active role-taking in which attitudes, not characters, are the chief concern.

Process drama shares some of the elements found in SI but uses them in a more complex, immediate and flexible format. It requires language to be used in meaningful, authentic situations, where the focus is on problem posing and resolution. Teachers are co-creators of the dramatic world, and the roles they adopt within this world enable them to diagnose the students' language skills and understanding, support their communicative efforts, model appropriate behaviors within the situation, question their thinking and extend and challenge their responses.

Explorations and encounters in process drama are never merely a series of brief exercises, but include a variety of strategies and modes of organization (O'Neill & Lambert, 1982; O'Neill, 1995). Situations can be developed episodically or in units to articulate different aspects of the dramatic world. This involves careful sequencing and layering of dramatic units or episodes, often in a non-linear way, to cumulatively extend and enrich the fictional context. The constitution of these episodes or units instantly entails structure, as the relationship between parts of the work which make it a true process. The process is much more complex than the linear or chronological sequencing of the segments like a chain of beads. It is more like linking them together into a web of meaning.

An example of process drama occurred when a group of American high school students in a Spanish class faced the following challenge during a three-hour workshop. They were asked to imagine that they were adult members of families who had agreed to accept street children from a South American city into their homes. In role as a welfare worker, the teacher thanked them for their kindness, and provided them with background information about the conditions under which these children lived. The students asked questions and were given photographs, newspaper reports, and statistics about the children's lives and the negative reaction of government agencies to their plight. These activities took place in English, the students' first language, as did the next stage of the lesson.

Working in groups in role as adults, the students "created" particular children whom they would agree to foster. Names, ages, and particular circumstances for the children were developed. Next, the students began to develop the kind of vocabulary that they felt they would need in welcoming the children to their homes. They wrote letters to the children in Spanish, describing their homes and the life that awaited the children there. This phase of the lesson corresponds to Di Pietro's rehearsal phase, in that students are anticipating and preparing for the linguistic demands that may arise later.

Now the students changed perspective, and, working in small groups, created a non-verbal frozen picture—a tableau—of a moment from the children's life on the streets. Although there was limited space in the classroom, each group in turn presented their tableau to the rest of the class in the available area at the front of the class. As the students watched each others' efforts, they found Spanish words to describe both the situation as they interpreted it, and what the children within the event might be thinking and feeling. Then they took the role of these children and wrote brief letters and journal entries in Spanish, describing their situation and their hopes for the future.

Next, the teacher selected several students whom she thought would be able to handle a more demanding kind of role-play. These students were asked to remain in the role of street children. The rest of the group returned to their roles as the charitable adults. The teacher explained that they had traveled to South America to meet the children. In groups of three or four, the adults interviewed the street children, to try to determine whether they would be suitable for fostering. The street children were instructed by the teacher to react in ways which made the encounter challenging for the adults. Some decided to be very shy or sullen, others were sick, frightened or alienated. The interview was conducted in Spanish, and the teacher, still in role as the social worker, was available to assist and support the students' efforts.

In the next episode of the drama, the students had to work more spontaneously in role in the target language without any outside assistance and in a situation of greater tension. The teacher took on the role of a Spanish-speaking government official, hostile to any plans to remove the street children, and very concerned to deny the extent of the children's problems. The students had to convince the official that the children were genuinely needy and that it would be beneficial to uproot them from their neighborhoods and take them to a foreign country. This encounter challenged all their resources, both social and linguistic. They had to remain sufficiently diplomatic to continue the conversation with the official and yet they had to insist that the government was neglecting these children. After a difficult first meeting, the issue remained unresolved. The students returned to their groups and prepared both the arguments and the vocabulary with which they might convince the official to allow them to remove the children. A second meeting was arranged with the official, who reluctantly agreed to look into the matter and see what could be done.

In the final phase of the drama, the teacher explained that 10 years had passed since the previous episode. The children were now young adults. Each group was asked to create a scene, including both dialogue and movement, that would show the decisions that had been taken, and what had happened to the particular child they had adopted. A variety of possibilities was displayed. In some cases, the child had not escaped from its environment, and had been either destroyed by it, or had risen above it. In one scene, a child had become a social worker, helping a new generation of street children to make better lives for themselves. In other scenes the children had gone to the United States, and either become educated and affluent, or remained outsiders in their new surroundings, alienated from their past and their homeland.

This sequence of activities included phases of preparation and rehearsal, written assignments, interviews, non-verbal representations, rehearsed scenes, and spontaneous encounters. The drama developed through an increasingly intense series of episodes or scenes, each one presenting the students with different linguistic and social challenges. The tension of the drama, and the need to overcome obstacles and to accomplish their mission produced commitment to the activity and a degree of fluency which surprised the students themselves.

The teacher functioned within the framework of the drama, taking on two distinct roles, each one presenting a different level of support or challenge for the students. In role as a social worker, the teacher introduced the issue in the students' first language, presented them with their task and supported them into an engagement in the topic. At the later stage, when the students were more deeply involved with the characters they had created in the drama, the teacher as the Spanish-speaking official was able to challenge their ability to convince a hostile adult of the validity of their opinions and to handle a problematic social situation. Both students and teacher shared responsibility for the whole sequence of activities.

The essential characteristics of process drama include the following:

1. Its purpose is to generate a dramatic "elsewhere," a fictional world, which will be inhabited for the experiences, insights, interpretations and understandings it may yield.
2. It does not proceed from a pre-written script or scenario, but rather from a theme, situation or pre-text that interests and challenges the participants.
3. It is built up from a series of episodes, which may be improvised or composed and rehearsed.
4. It takes place over a time span that allows this kind of elaboration.
5. It involves the whole group in the same enterprise.
6. There is no external audience to the event, but participants are audience to their own acts.

Process drama shares some qualities with SI, but goes further in its emphasis on immediacy, involvement, student autonomy and teacher functions. The key aspects of process drama are summarized as follows:

The *objectives* of process drama in the second language classroom are to increase the fluency and confidence of the students' speech, to create authentic communication contexts, and to generate new classroom relationships. The activity usually involves *large groups* or *the whole class* at the initial stage and is likely to involve *small-group* and *pair work* as the drama continues. The context is likely to be launched by the "*teacher in role*" and developed with the students' input. The roles created in the work are general at first but later become specific and individualized at the students' own discretion. *Tensions* arise from the dramatic situation and the intentions of the roles. The *teacher* participates in the process of developing the drama in

Drama Approaches Key Aspects	Closed Communication	Semi-Controlled	Open Communication
Objectives	1. accuracy 2. practice 3. confidence	1. fluency 2. practice 3. authority 4. challenge	1. fluency 2. authenticity 3. confidence 4. challenge 5. new classroom rela- tion
Organization	1. pair work 2. small groups 3. rehearsal	1. small groups 2. some rehearsal 3. unpredictable end- ing	1. usually begins with large group 2. pair work and small groups as work con- tinues
Context	1. simple 2. naturalistic 3. teacher selected	1. determined by stu- dents in consulta- tion with teacher	1. launched by teacher in role 2. developed with stu- dents' input
Roles	1. individual 2. teacher determined 3. fixed attitudes	1. group members 2. spokepersons groups 3. individual role-tak- ing	1. generalized at first 2. becoming individu- alized at students' own choice later
Decisions	1. none	1. determined by stu- dents	1. negotiated by stu- dents
Tension	1. to produce accuracy of language and vocabulary	1. arising from the social dynamic rather than a focus on accuracy	1.arising from the dra- matic situation and the intentions of the roles
Teacher Functions	1. to set up exercises 2. to provide resource 3. to be evaluator	1. to initiate 2. to support 3. to provide resource	1. in role 2. as model 3. to support 4. to provide resource 5. to challenge

FIGURE 1.2. Summary of the differences in key aspects of three drama approaches

role with the students and *functions* as a model, support, and resource for the students' efforts. During the process it is possible for the teacher to extend and challenge the ideas and language ability of the students.

MOTIVATION AND INVOLVEMENT IN PROCESS DRAMA

When students are able to include some part of themselves in what is happening in the classroom, they are more likely to participate in that process (Di Pietro, 1982a). In creating and maintaining the worlds that arise in process drama, students construct and explore images, roles, ideas, and situations. They learn to manipulate language in order to bring life to people, places and events which do not exist. They share their understanding with the rest of the group, allowing them to further shape ideas, feelings and attitudes which might otherwise remain wholly private and unavailable.

A classroom in which drama is used as a way into language learning will demonstrate some special qualities. Students will feel they have a voice; they will interact with each other and the teacher in new ways; the classroom discourse will be both dialogic and democratic. Students do not merely play roles but create roles and transcend them. When language structures and interaction patterns change, so does the content of what is being said. The students have a standpoint from which to communicate their thoughts, feelings and opinions. They also have the authority to put these into words. They are both creating and maintaining the dramatic event through authentic language.

The kind of pedagogy elicited by the use of process drama in L2 teaching is an essentially liberating one. Its qualities relate closely to the characteristics of the kind of liberating education advocated by Friere (1972). These characteristics include

1. participation;
2. cooperation;
3. posing problems;
4. the validation of students' ideas for classroom content and discourse;
5. students' control over the learning process;
6. learners working in community, cooperating and pooling their resources;
7. the teachers' creativity;
8. reflection;
9. self and peer evaluation; and
10. a sense of coherence.

As Bruner (1986) makes clear in "Actual Minds, Possible Worlds," an ideal education partakes of the spirit of a forum, negotiation, and the recreation of meaning. He claims that education can become part of culture making. L2 teachers have always seen an induction into the culture of the target language as part of their endeavors, and drama allows them to achieve this objective.

SUMMARY

This chapter offers an account of the key advantages of using drama approaches in the L2 classroom. A brief outline of the development of drama in education and its effects in the broader curriculum is included. We have considered examples of three different drama approaches and isolated the key features of each. Each approach has been placed on a continuum from closed to open communication. In the next chapter, we focus on critical elements in creating effective drama in the L2 classroom.

2

Evoking Dramatic Moments in Second Language Classrooms

INTRODUCTION

I f the primary approach to teach a second language is to promote open communication by involving students in drama, an immediate challenge arises: How do teachers create effective drama activities in the classroom and achieve their objectives for learners of different levels? To face this challenge, three questions need to be addressed:

1. What is effective drama?
2. What are the critical elements in creating effective drama?
3. How can these elements be planned for and later implemented in the actual classroom?

Using process drama to teach a second language is more complex than using any other kind of drama activity because this approach is flexible and unpredictable. Many variables arise when participants bring their individual experience and understanding to this collaborative process.

However, creating an effective L2 drama classroom is not as difficult as many teachers think, once they thoroughly understand the nature of process drama. In this chapter, our discussion will focus on these three questions in order to clarify how to evoke dramatic moments in an L2 classroom.

THE NATURE AND FUNCTIONS OF PROCESS DRAMA

During the discussion in the previous chapter, we established that in an L2 classroom process drama offers

1.   new contexts;
2.   different roles, attitudes and perspectives;
3.   democratic classroom relationships;
4.   a range of language opportunities; and
5.   access to current cultural aspects.

Process drama involves creating and articulating an improvised dramatic event. Participants are required to generate, manipulate and transform the elements of the process. They control significant aspects of the event because they simultaneously experience it and create it. They also evaluate what is happening and make connections to the real world and to their own lives. Drama demands perception, imagination, speculation and interpretation from the participants, and exercises their cognitive, linguistic and social capacities, even when they are using their native language.

In the L2 classroom the key to the effectiveness lies in the creation of an immediate and unpredictable social context. All encounters among participants within this fictional context will promote meaningful and purposeful language use. Once the dramatic world begins to grow, the usual classroom context is replaced by new contexts, roles and relationships among students and also between the students and teachers. The patterns of communication and interaction in the classroom are fundamentally altered, generating unique possibilities of social, personal, and linguistic development. The focus is on the interactions and encounters among the participants, rather than on the accuracy of their speech. Instead, fluency springs from the motivation to communicate within the dramatic situation and from the emphasis on meaning. Students involved in the rich variety of speech events that drama promotes draw on all their linguistic and paralinguistic resources as they struggle to communicate. Because the talk that arises in drama is embedded in context, it is purposeful and essentially generative.

Traditional classroom discourse, even when conducted in the students' native tongue, rarely offers opportunities for the exploration of a range of complex language functions, since these functions arise from personal, sustained, and intensive encounters. The teacher's functions include sustaining intensive interaction with students and structuring complex and authentic language learning environments. In the majority of classrooms, this function is almost always limited to highly controlled teacher/student interactions. The limitation on sustained and fruitful interactions with students is even more marked in L2 classrooms. The teacher may model, support and prompt the students' skills and operate as resource, coach and consultant, but will rarely have the opportunity to stimulate and challenge the students' emerging competence.

For the teacher wishing to use process drama, there are a number of implications that have to be accepted in the classroom:

1. Language is not only a cognitive activity, but also an intensely social and personal endeavor;
2. Both students and teachers must be prepared to take risks and take alternatives within a functioning speech community;
3. The teacher can no longer presume to dominate the learning, and should be prepared to function in a variety of ways, including taking on a role within the drama.

From the above discussion, some conclusions emerge. First, the way in which the drama begins is critical in the development of successful follow-up activities. The contexts chosen will determine the authenticity of the drama and thus influence the students' involvement levels. Carefully selecting a wide range of roles for students is also important because it allows the students to explore the drama world and helps them to go beyond the restricted classroom roles they usually inhabit. "Teacher in role" is a unique and effective strategy for launching process drama. With this strategy, the teacher can become involved in the activity, challenge the students with authentic questions, yet retain some control in developing the work. Questioning is another useful strategy available to the teacher to help set up the parameters of the fictional world.

While negotiating the roles, scenes and meanings, participants arrive at a deeper understanding of the drama. When the above elements are present, dramatic tension will arise. This tension will promote the intellectual and emotional engagement of the students and increase the power of the drama. Last but not least, it is critical to allow the students to reflect upon what has happened because reflection enables them to become aware of the learning they have achieved. In the following sections we will discuss each of these elements in detail and how they can be implemented effectively.

INTRODUCING PROCESS DRAMA

When drama activities such as role-plays or scenarios are introduced to students, the teacher typically sets the assignment, gives instructions, suggests roles, and monitors the results. The task of setting up a sequence of episodes in process drama is rather more complex. Because the work requires structure and yet allows for spontaneous responses as it develops over time, it is essential to find a starting point that intrigues and involves students. This starting point should rapidly enlist the students' language and imagination in creating the fictional world that will emerge through the drama.

There are a variety of effective ways of launching a drama sequence and generating a fruitful context. In the Street Children lesson described in the previous chapter, students were invited to invent the name, personality, and background of a homeless South American child. The responsibility they took in completing this task, the fact that the imaginary child was their own creation, and the level of control they exercised at the beginning of the work were the key factors in keeping them engaged in the more challenging episodes of the drama. Studies indicate that a degree of control over the situation generated from the student group will produce optimum results for L2 learners in listening and speaking (Johnson, 1988). Another way of achieving a similar result might have been to show the students a number of photographs and have them use these images as a basis for their invention. Pictorial representations are familiar in L2 teaching. They help students build vocabulary by naming and describing items, answering questions or developing a story. Images may be used in a more dynamic way to generate a problem that needs solving within a fictional world.

A visiting researcher, involved in a project in a Spanish immersion school, used a map depicting a community to initiate process drama with first-graders. He explained that a dog had been lost and enlisted the help of the children to find it. They questioned their Spanish-speaking teacher, who was in role as the dog's owner, searched for clues, and eventually found the dog. They were then challenged by the researcher, in another role, who claimed the dog belonged to him. The children eventually solved the problem and returned the dog to its owner (Bernhardt, 1992).

Useful starting points for drama occur in all kinds of sources. Myths, legends, novels, and short stories will provide ideas and issues, especially if these texts involve people who have to make decisions or solve problems. These sources as well as plots from classic drama can be used as "pre-texts," which will provide "atmosphere, situations, tensions, tasks and dilemmas" (O'Neill, 1995, p. 37). Di Pietro (1982a) suggested that headlines or letters in the daily newspaper, works of literature chosen from the target language, as well as the real-life experiences of the participants may provide authentic themes for drama work.

The kind of starting-point that is chosen and the way in which it evolves will depend on the age of the students, their competence in the target language, and the teacher's learning objectives. For example, as part of a research project in a French immersion elementary school, fifth-grade students became young athletes invited to attend an international Youth Olympics (Bernhardt, 1992). Speaking in English, the researcher, in role as an Olympic official, congratulated them on being chosen for the American team, and explained that they would be traveling to France for the Games and would need some practice in French as they would have to communicate in a number of different situations. First, the students prepared a short piece of pantomime in which they displayed the athletic skill for which they had been selected. This non-verbal activity was enjoyable for students of this age, although it might not be appropriate for adolescents or adult learners. The whole class watched each student in turn and provided the vocabulary to describe what was happening. Next, each student prepared a visa document in French. This was in fact a rehearsal phase, in which essential vocabulary was introduced by the teacher. This preparation was followed by an episode in which there was considerable tension. They had to face the teacher, a native speaker of French, in role as a French immigration officer. Each "athlete" was questioned in considerable depth about various details on their visa application, including such facts as their names, ages, addresses, schools, and purpose of traveling. Many of these basic details had been practiced as part of language drills in their regular classroom activities, but now the students had the opportunity to recall and use them in a far more authentic setting under pressure from a very bureaucratic official. Later episodes in this drama included tableaux of various moments from the Games, showing both triumphs and disasters, as well as interviews with a French journalist—the teacher in another questioning role—but this time a more sympathetic one. Written assignments ranged from an imaginary diary of the trip, to letters and postcards sent from France to their friends and relatives, and newspaper headlines about their successes at the Olympic Games. In this sequence the roles, played by students and teachers, allowed them to ask and answer questions, interpret responses, pose and solve problems, work in movement and speech, and react appropriately and resourcefully within the fictional situation and the target language.

CONTEXTS

The contexts that are chosen for drama may include serious "realistic" situations, for example, street children, lost dogs, or environmental concerns; aspirational themes, such as Olympic athletes or famous people; contexts familiar to the students like school trips; and even subjects that seem totally fantastic, such as talking animals on a TV show or the trial of the Big Bad Wolf. The particular choice of context will be determined by the students' social skills and cultural understanding as much as by their language ability. Younger students are likely to respond easily and immediately to the "make believe" offered by process drama. Adolescents may need a realistic approach in order to overcome negative attitudes and help them perceive the usefulness of drama. Once they have adjusted to an unfamiliar method, it will be possible to extend the range of contexts to include more imaginative approaches. Initially, adults may feel more secure in a context that is playful rather than serious, so that they feel free to take risks and make mistakes. We offer practical examples in Chapter Three. A context that is obviously far removed from everyday concerns can offer a light-hearted, playful atmosphere, in which exploration and enjoyment are the primary purposes and the lack of pressure to produce a "correct" speech promotes confidence and fluency.

ROLES

Individual Roles

All kinds of dramatic activity, from the professional performance on stage to pretend play in which the child engage, is the direct result of our human capacity to manipulate and transform the roles we inhabit (O'Neill, 1995). Through drama, we can transcend our limited and restrictive social roles, and discover new aspects of our personality. In L2 teaching, the initial purpose of endowing students with different roles will be to provide them with fresh linguistic possibilities. In typical teacher-controlled role-play, these roles are likely to be restricted by the teacher's didactic purposes. However, even if the roles available to students are primarily functional, they may offer some small degree of self-transcendence—something that goes beyond the here and now of the real classroom situation. In the example outlined earlier, the students as young Olympic athletes used the actual details of their lives, their names, ages, and schools to build up their roles but added the extremely significant fictional element of being outstanding in one area of athletics.

For Heathcote, one of the most important aspects of taking on a role is its spontaneity (Johnson & O'Neill, 1984). It is this quality that constantly surprises individuals into the discovery of their own competencies. She claims that her purpose in drama is to release students into a new awareness of what they already know but do not yet realize they know. Moreno, a pioneer in the use of role-play in therapy, emphasized the importance of spontaneity in distinguishing two major manifestations of role. The first was "role taking," the enactment of a situation in a totally predetermined manner. Many exercises in L2 teaching fall into this category. Moreno's second category was "role creating," which demands both creativity and spontaneity in responding appropriately to the given circumstances (Moreno, 1959). This spontaneity is also central to the adoption of roles in process drama.

It is possible for the L2 teacher to give students the widest possible opportunities for language use by endowing them with carefully chosen roles that go far beyond their usual restricted classroom roles. The most useful roles will be those that permit students to ask and answer questions, to solve problems, to offer both information and opinions, to argue and persuade, and generally to fulfill the widest range of language functions.

Group Roles

One of the ways in which process drama differs from more conventional kinds of improvisation and role-play is in the kinds of roles available to students. In simple role-plays students are likely to be given a limited individual role, for example, a dissatisfied customer making a complaint or a tourist asking directions. Attitudes are strictly determined and functionally adapted to the situation. In the SI approach, (Di Pietro, 1987a) a group of students will take responsibility during the rehearsal phase for anticipating and preparing for an interaction with a particular role. In contrast, in process drama students are likely to be initially endowed with a kind of group or generic role; that is, they all begin the drama as the same type of person. They are defined, at least at first, by their roles as members of a particular group involved in a special enterprise or circumstance, holding a particular attitude or with a specific task to perform. Examples include the charitable people in the Street Children lesson from Chapter One, as well as the young athletes described in this chapter. A very rough idea and some general background information about the role—for example, a street child in a South American city, or a young athlete going to France for the youth Games—are provided to the students. The students then work in groups to "shape" this role further through discussion and activities. The role each group creates gradually differs from those generated by other groups in characteristics, personal background, talents, attitudes to society, experience in the past, perspectives toward the future and consequences in life as the drama unfolds. This group role provides tremendous support for L2 students to overcome insecurities as well as their incompetence in using the target language at this initial stage of making drama.

Every individual response from members of the group belongs, in a sense, to everyone who is part of that group. Less competent students can still be part of the activity without exposing their lack of skill and confidence. For students who are unfamiliar with this way of working, a group role provides an initial perspective on the unfolding situation, and each individual can join in at the level of their own linguistic competence. Their contribution of even a single word or a simple phrase will make them part of the event, and will signal their entitlement to bring their ideas to the developing action.

When students are in role in this way, they are not required to "act," like an actor on stage, but instead to adopt particular attitudes and perspectives and respond appropriately. As they do so, they are at the same time an audience to the performances of their peers and the teacher as they engage in the drama. This demands a level of listening and comprehension from participants as they adapt their input to what has already been said. As Heathcote emphasizes, one cannot force people to adopt a commitment to a particular point of view, but if they are put in a position to respond, they begin to hold a point of view because they can see that it has power (Johnson & O'Neill, 1984). The teacher's language, especially if the teacher is "in role," will provide both a model and a support for their efforts.

TEACHER IN ROLE

"Teacher in role" is one of the most effective ways of beginning process drama. It is a hallmark of the process and clearly distinguishes it from other more limited approaches. We have provided several examples of this strategy, where the teacher takes on a role and enters the developing action of the drama. The willingness of the teacher to enter and build the fictional world in this way is a powerful means of altering the atmosphere, relationships and balance of power in the classroom, since it immediately changes the function of the teacher within the lesson. In more traditional creative drama lessons, the teacher typically remains an external facilitator, a side coach, a director or a "loving ally," rather than working within the drama in role. "Teacher in role" is closely identified with the work of Dorothy Heathcote, who was the first to develop the strategy systematically.

The initial purpose of taking on a role is emphatically not to give a display of acting, but to invite students to enter and begin to create the fictional world. When the teacher takes on a role in the interaction, it is an act of conscious self-presentation, and one that invites the students to respond actively, to join in and to extend, oppose or transform what is happening. It sends out signals to students that the activity is regarded seriously by the teacher, and that input from both teacher and students is equally valid. For Gavin Bolton, teacher in role is the most important and subtle strategy in the drama teacher's repertoire. It is both a strategy for learning and a significant principle of teaching, which uniquely inverts the assumptions underlying the traditional pedagogical context. The power relationship between pupils and teacher is tacitly perceived as negotiable.

The advantages of working in role for the teacher are manifold. This strategy makes it possible for the teacher to establish the imaginary situation briefly and economically, without lengthy explanations and assigning of parts, model appropriate behavior and language, maintain the dramatic tension and challenge and support the students from within the fictional situation. Criteria of possibility are set up and appropriate conventions of language and behavior are seen in action. Through the use of "teacher in role," it is possible to bind the participants together as a group, engage them immediately in the dramatic action, and manipulate language. The teacher is never merely "acting" or joining in on equal terms with the group. That would be to overlook the key educational and structural aspects of the strategy. The teacher in role has a different task which is to bring the students into active participation in the event.

The possible functions of the teacher are multiplied by using teacher in role. Whether in the first or second language classroom, this complex approach operates to focus the attention of the participants, harness their feelings of ambivalence and vulnerability, unite them in contemplation and engage them in action. The role presented by the teacher is publicly available to be "read" or interpreted, and participants are immediately caught in a web of contemplation, speculation and anticipation. They are drawn together in attending to and building the event, as they seek for clues to the kind of fictional world that is emerging and their place within it. Students are challenged to make sense of what they hear and see, to become aware of their responses and to use these responses as an impetus to action. They are invited not only to enter the dramatic world but to transform it; not merely to take on roles but to create and transcend them.

A rehearsal phase can be built in as part of the action. All of the students can be involved in the situation at once, for example where all the students consult about the best way to find the lost dog or to persuade the obstructive official. The situation becomes increasingly authentic, yet is still occurring in, as Heathcote calls, a ludic "no penalty" area (Johnson & O'Neill, 1984, p. 165). It is the role, not the teacher, who responds to any communication or opposition from the class, so both teacher and students are protected by the fictional nature of the event.

TENSION

Another key characteristic of process drama, and one that distinguishes it from simple role-plays, is that at its most effective, it operates through the tension generated within the situation. Tension has the dictionary definition of "mental excitement," and has been defined by drama educators in the following ways:

1. Morgan and Saxton (1987) make clear that "a mental excitement is fundamental to intellectual and emotional engagement, not only as a stimulus, but as the bonding agent that sustains involvement in the dramatic task" (p. 3).
2. The tension of the moment in every interaction, as Di Pietro (1987a) recognized, evokes language and helps it to be retained.

Tension is a key quality in drama, whether improvised or scripted, although it has not always been recognized as such. Too often in theater and drama, the much cruder notion of "conflict" is seen as the dynamic force in drama. Viola Spolin, author of the immensely influential "Improvisation for the Theater," identifies the weakness of this view when she defines conflict as a "device for generating stage energy" (Spolin, 1963, p. 379). Tension, on the other hand, is an essential structural principle in generating dramatic worlds. Momentum can only develop if a state of tension is created that provides a dynamic for the action. Tension is an essential aesthetic element, closely linked with such qualities as time and rhythm. It exists between the situation as it appears at any one moment and the complete action. Tension can be created in theater by the ignorance of the characters and the knowledge of the audience about elements of the action. For example, the tension in *Romeo and Juliet* increases to the maximum when the audience see Romeo drinking the poison in the tomb beside his lover's body, because the audience are clear that Juliet is not really dead. Romeo, as the hero in the play does not know this. In other cases tension is created, as Di Pietro (1987a) suggested in "Strategic Interactions," by the struggle between the intentions of one role and another. For example in one scenario suggested by Di Pietro, the tension arises when the flower shop keeper intends to get rid of the not-so-fresh flowers first but the customer shows more interest in fresh ones (1987a, p. 28). Tension is never merely suspense, waiting for something to happen, but implies both pressure and resistance. It arises as much from what is known as from what is unknown. The students wishing to rescue the street children in our example described earlier are in no doubt that the official will oppose their plans. The tension arises as they struggle to overcome objections to their plans. It comes from within the situation. It is a result not only of what is already apprehended but of what is anticipated. Dramatic tension of this kind keeps any play, game or dramatic interaction alive.

Traditional language exercises are typically set up in order to *remove* any tension, so that repetition and eventually accuracy will occur. Their value lies in the fact that they isolate a particular factor and allow attention to be focused on it. As Heathcote puts it, "when drama is exercise-driven, the natural discoveries that come from emotional involvement cannot arise" (Johnson & O'Neill, 1984, p. 98).

How does tension arise in drama? Some of the most effective dramas are evoked by the teacher asking a question or setting a problem for the students. Effective questioning will be the teacher's most important tool, both at the beginning of the drama, and at critical moments within the interactions. Encounters with the teacher in role are also likely to produce tension, particularly if the role presented appears ambiguous, obstructive or untrustworthy. For students, interpreting the possible intentions of such a role and responding appropriately is a source of immediate tension within the group.

Different levels of tension will operate in drama, depending on the context and the teacher's purposes, but without this essential dramatic and interactional element, the drama is unlikely to develop effectively. Tension may arise from direct confrontation, as a way of harnessing the energy or resistance of the class; it may appear more subtly as a dilemma, a veiled threat, a pressure posed by an outside agency, or by such factors as a time pressure which demands a rapid response. At times, such tensions may reveal themselves immediately; at others, they may emerge as the drama develops and the issues at stake become clear. As the drama proceeds, one tension may replace another. Examples of this occurred in the Lost Dog lesson, where the initial tension of finding the dog was replaced by a need to prove its true ownership or in the Street Children drama when the pressure to relate successfully with these alienated youngsters is succeeded by the need to overcome the objections of the official.

NEGOTIATION

In *Learning Through Drama* by McGregor, Tate, and Robinson (1977), drama was defined as the negotiation of meaning. Drama cannot happen without negotiation between teacher and class and among students. Similarly, language use is regarded by Widdowson (1990) as essentially a matter of negotiating meaning. In linguistics, negotiation is seen as a higher level skill yet students with the lowest level of communication skills can negotiate if there is opportunity and motivation (Lantolf & Khanji, 1982). As Heathcote puts it, the whole negotiation of role involves a "delicate linguistics," as well as the ability to use gesture and space significantly (Johnson & O'Neill, 1984). Every phase of the drama will require negotiation, although it is likely to be particularly evident at the beginning of the process, as students and teachers seek to define the parameters of the emerging fictional world.

Negotiation will also occur among students as they work in smaller groups, prepare for a dramatic activity or rehearse an item for presentation to the class. These negotiations will challenge their social skills as well as their linguistic capacities, but these demands are an essential justification for using this approach.

NON-VERBAL ACTIVITIES

Although the purpose of using drama in the L2 classroom is to generate language, the inclusion of non-verbal episodes within the process can be very valuable. Di Pietro (1983) noted that second language teaching methods make little effort to address gestural communication and the kind of non-verbal episode that can easily be incorporated into the drama. Perhaps the most useful non-verbal technique in process drama is the "tableau," "still picture," or "freeze frame." Students, working in small groups, prepare an image of some kind and present it to the rest of the class, as, for example, the "pictures" created by students to show the lives of the street children (see "Street Children" example in Chapter One). These images are created and interpreted in order to provide information, gain insight, or acquire understanding about a particular situation. The selective use of a tableau within process drama releases students from the demands of an immediate linguistic response, slows down the action, requires co-operation and composition, embodies understanding, and allows a level of abstraction. For example, creating a tableau of a statue commemorating the street children can help participants recollect their understanding about the "Street Children" theme without verbal expressions and arrive at a conclusion of their own at the end of the series of episodes. This is also the most powerful uses of tableau: to inspire reflection within or beyond the drama.

Mime or pantomime is a more familiar procedure to most L2 teachers. It is usually performed individually, and this makes it more suitable for younger students who may not be inhibited by such exposure. Again, working in mime releases students from the constraints of language. In other words, mime is an alternative for L2 learners at lower competence levels to express their thoughts with their body and not in the language that they are yet comfortable with. The mimes they produce demand an economy of expression and, like tableaux develop an awareness of the significance of spatial representation. Without the help of verbal expressions, the students need to use their physical movements very carefully to get their ideas across without causing any misunderstanding or ambiguity. Both techniques provide opportunities for building vocabulary, developing roles, providing information, testing understanding and promoting reflection.

It is important that non-verbal approaches do not turn into mere "guessing games," where the group expends its energies on trying to decipher what is happening in the tableau or mime, rather than interrogating the images or sequence of gestures for the meanings they contain.

QUESTIONING

Teachers spend a large proportion of their time asking questions of their students. Much of the time, however, these questions are not "authentic," in that the teacher already knows the answer, and is merely checking the students' knowledge. Questioning in drama works very differently. Often it is the teacher's questions that help to give students a sense of their roles and establish the parameters of the fictional world. The teacher is dependent upon the students' answers in order to move the drama forward. As Morgan and Saxton (1987) put it, "questions are first and foremost an opportunity for clarifying and testing out meaning and understanding" (p. 83).

Skillful questioning within the drama process can strengthen students' commitment to their roles, supply information indirectly, model the appropriate language register, focus their linguistic efforts, remodel inaccurate responses, and deepen students' thinking about the issues involved in the drama. For example, in the Street Children drama, the teacher in role, as an obstructive official, was able to confront the students' beliefs that the best thing to do for the children was to remove them from their native environment. At the same time, the official's questions were an important element in creating tension, and this is one of the most useful functions of questioning. Drama topics or roles that allow the students themselves to ask questions are especially useful in giving them a sense of control and ownership of the work. The teacher's questioning is likely to be particularly significant during the reflective phase of the lesson, but throughout the drama it will always be more important to generate significant questions than to demand right answers.

REFLECTION

Reflection on what has happened in the lesson is a key way of eliciting trust and developing commitment to the process (Johnson & O'Neill, 1984). For Heathcote, the explicit educational aim of her work in drama is always to build a reflective and contemplative attitude in the participants. It is only in recent years that Heathcote's emphasis on learning and reflection, the immediacy and significance of the experience, and its essential group nature have become common currency among drama teachers.

Reflection is a way of making students' aware of the learning that has taken place and demonstrating the significance of their achievements, both socially and linguistically. These may not always be obvious, as the energy and enjoyment of the process may mask a genuine growth in fluency and confidence. Where the drama has not been immediately successful, reflection can save a situation from degenerating still further. It will allow the teacher to clarify objectives, reframe tasks, invite students' questions and take steps to repair students' self-esteem. Reflection serves a variety of purposes. It can be used to review progress, prepare for the next stage of the drama, discover students' thoughts and feelings about the content or form of the work, resolve problems, and evaluate skills. Discussion of such topics needs to be skillfully handled. Sometimes the most effective discussions can take place inside the drama, and reflection does not always need to be carried out discursively. In the Street Children lesson, for example, reflection on students' feelings as they work through the structure could be achieved by adding a further phase to the lesson in which the teacher in role as a journalist questions them in their first language about their experiences. The sole purpose of this kind of role is to engage students in reflective talk about their responses within the drama. To reflect non-verbally on the whole theme of the work, the class might be asked to work in small groups and create a "statue" of the street children, to be set up in a place where it might help to remind the public of the ordeals they had overcome in their lives.

Reflection can be achieved through extending the drama into other activities and other expressive modes. Heathcote uses the contrasting energies of non-dramatic activities such as writing, drawing and map-making to enrich and deepen the quality of reflection on the dramatic experience. Writing in role is a very motivating task, since students have a great deal to draw on. Letters, diaries, drawings, maps, plans, newspaper headlines, official reports, obituaries and so on may all be used to extend their involvement in the drama, deepen their responses and offer a variety of further language opportunities, both formal and informal.

Probably the most frequent use of reflection in the L2 classroom is to comment on and correct students' linguistic errors. This is obviously a priority for L2 teachers, but an over-emphasis on these evaluative aspects may have a negative effect on students' future involvement in the work. Such comments need to be handled positively by focusing on what the students have achieved. Suggestions for alternative idioms or vocabulary to improve communication can be solicited from the rest of the class, or provided by the teacher. It will be important to discuss, not just what individual students have contributed to the drama, but also what they felt within the experience and their responses to the challenges that arose.

SUMMARY

In this chapter, we have considered some of the key elements in creating effective process drama. To use process drama successfully in the L2 classroom, the teacher needs to be able to undertake the following functions:

1. Find an effective starting point for the drama, and if necessary, initiate the drama in role.
2. Choose themes and topics appropriate for the social and linguistic abilities of the students.
3. Introduce a variety of roles in order to familiarize students with a wide range of language functions.
4. Understand and foster the operation of tension in the dramatic situation, so that encounters continue to be unpredictable and authentic.
5. Handle the class as a whole group as well as organizing students into pairs and small groups.
6. Release students from the constraints of language and provide them with fresh opportunities by incorporating non-verbal activities in the process.
7. Negotiate the development of the drama with students, and encourage similar positive interactions among students.
8. Use a variety of forms of questioning to promote involvement, support students' contributions and challenge superficial or inadequate responses.
9. Reflect on the experience, both in discussion and through the use of other modes of expression.
10. Extend the drama experience beyond the limits of the classroom by making connections with society and with the students' own lives.

3

The Nature of
Teacher-Student Interaction
in Drama-Oriented
Language Classrooms

INTRODUCTION

Various drama techniques have long been popular among language teachers in teaching a second language. However, conducting valid and reliable research about what is happening in drama-oriented language classrooms has been neglected by language teachers and researchers. The question arising from this trend is: How can the use of drama approaches be justified in classroom practice without strong support from research findings?

The intention of this chapter is twofold. First, we explore the main characteristics of teachers' and students' verbal interaction in L2 classrooms in general and in drama activities in particular. Second, we explain the relationship between the participants' discourse experience in drama and their learning process, based on empirical evidence obtained from recent classroom studies.

THE CLASSROOM AS A UNIQUE WORLD OF
COMMUNICATION

Participating in real-life conversations requires sophisticated skills in verbal and behavioral communication: adopting different roles, performing various tasks, using appropriate forms of language, finding suitable forms of social behavior, and so on. Native speakers acquire these skills by observing and imitating people around them from the very beginning of their lives. These skills are then gradually mastered through constant trial and error in different contexts during the course of growing up. Even so, native speakers may still encounter frustration and misunderstanding in their everyday communication. This is because a conversation is a dialogue. It cannot be constructed by a single speaker (that would be a monologue). It needs effort and input contributed by at least two parties.

Adolescent and adult L2 learners often feel that they already know how to communicate with people because of their experience of their mother tongue. They tend to believe that they can participate naturally in any daily conversation after they have learned the basic structures and forms of the target language in the classroom. This rather naive view of human communication underestimates the complexity and difficulty of controlling a discourse in context, especially when different cultures meet. In fact, successfully communicating intended meanings in one's native language is far more complicated than many people imagine, not to mention conversing in a second language that has not yet been mastered. Kasper states the situation clearly: "Speaking a language means more than referring to the world, it also means relating to one's interlocutors" (Kasper, 1979, p. 395). In other words, putting one's entire effort into speaking does not guarantee a successful conversation. Only if one pays full attention to the interlocutor's utterances and then responds promptly and appropriately, can one convey meaning in real life communication.

Since there are so many factors involved in building a conversation in the real world, there are major obstacles for L2 learners to overcome in the formal school environment. It has been demonstrated that teacher-student interaction in a typical classroom setting does not reflect the complex phases of real-life communication. Studies of classroom interaction, in both first and second language settings, suggest that the classroom is a world of its own. In this micro world, teachers and students communicate according to unique rules and conventions that are distinctively different from those used in the outside world (van Lier, 1984a).

As early as the 1960s, Bellack and associates (1966) noticed that in order to achieve certain educational goals, utterances produced by teachers and students carry non-linguistic functions in the classroom. Bellack and colleagues analyzed how teachers and students talk, based on the theory of "utterances as actions" proposed by Austin (1962) (the "Speech Act" theory), and worked out a system of pedagogical moves from their observations. Their study suggests that the teaching cycle is formed by the following four moves: *structuring*, *soliciting*, *responding*, and *reacting*. The teaching cycle goes as follows: the teacher structures the class by giving some direction to the students (e.g., "Turn to Lesson Two."), asks a question (e.g., "What is this man doing in the picture?"), and once the students respond to the question (e.g., "He is watching TV."), evaluates the response (e.g., "Good!").

Sinclair and Coulthard (1975) further investigated the transactions that make up lessons in primary-school mother-tongue content classes. They found a basic exchange structure between the teacher and students: teacher *Initiation*-pupil *Response*-teacher *Follow* or *Feedback* (or known as I-R-F structure). Take the following dialogue, for example:

Teacher:	It's a saw, yes this is a saw. What do we do with a saw?
Pupils:	Cut wood.
Teacher:	Yes. You're shouting though. What do we do with a saw?
Pupils:	Cut wood.
Teacher:	We cut wood. And, erm, what do we do with a hacksaw, this hacksaw?
Pupils:	Cut trees.
Teacher:	Do we cut trees with this?
Pupils:	No. No.
Teacher:	Hands up. What do we do with this?
Pupils:	Cut wood.
Teacher:	Do we cut wood with this?
Pupils:	No.
Teacher:	What do we do with that then?
Pupils:	Cut wood.
Teacher:	We cut wood with that. What do we do with that?
Pupil 1:	Sir.
Teacher:	Cleveland.
Pupil 1:	Metal.
Teacher:	We cut metal. Yes we cut metal. And er . . . (etc.).

(Data from Sinclair and Coulthard, 1975, pp. 93–94)   (3.1)

In this dialogue, the teacher is instructing the class about the functions of different tools. She initiates questions like "What do we do with this?" and the students respond to the questions as requested. The teacher then provides positive feedback, such as "Yes" and "Yes we cut metal," or negative feedback, such as asking the class several times "Do we cut trees with this?" to indicate that their previous answers are not acceptable. The teacher also controls the proceeding of the interaction by appointing a certain student to speak (such as "Cleveland") or changing the focus of the talk (e.g., "And erm, what do we do with a hacksaw?"). This dialogue, although a very short one, authentically reflects how teacher-student talk is constructed in many traditional classrooms. In this type of classroom, students rarely challenge the teacher but take it for granted that they must respond to their teachers' questions. Another problem with this kind of interaction is that the questions that are raised are seldom genuine.

Some may argue that students do have opportunities to "initiate" questions in the classroom. For example,

Teacher: Any question about Spain?
Student A: (Raises his hand)
Teacher: Yes, Bill?
Student A: Do they have subways there?
Teacher: Good question! Class, Bill has noticed the transportation system in Spain.   (3.2)

In this dialogue, Student A seems to initiate a question but his utterance is, in fact, a response to the teacher's previous invitation. Moreover, the teacher does not forget to evaluate the student's question before providing an appropriate answer (e.g., "good question"). Here, the teacher is still the initiator and evaluator of classroom conversation and the teacher-student exchange pattern in this dialogue does not greatly differ from that of the previous example. Sinclair and Coulthard (1975) suggest that one reason for this sequence is the unequal power distribution in the classroom where the teacher is socially superior to the students and therefore has the authority to initiate discourse and to judge other participants' contribution. Another possible reason for this sequence is that students—even much older ones—do not possess enough knowledge about the subject to "compete" with the teacher in the class. Take Dialogue 3.1 as an example. In this class, the teacher is the "knower" who is familiar with the functions of all the tools that are displayed; the students are obviously less knowledgeable than the teacher in this aspect. Under these circumstances it seems impossible for the students to have the same initiative as the teacher when the teacher is superior to the students in both social status and knowledge about the subject.

Studies of teacher's and students' behavior in L2 settings confirm that classroom interaction is traditionally controlled by the teacher. Holmes (1978) points out that the discourse relationship between the teacher and students is asymmetrical. It was found that teachers talk for around 70 percent of the time, control turn-taking by taking a superior stance similar to that of a chairperson in a formal meeting, and determine discourse topics by posing questions to students. Gremmo, Holec, and Riley (1978) also found that teachers generally perform twice as many "acts" as students do in L2 classrooms. Teachers open and close interaction exchanges, while students are restricted to replying; teachers elicit questions, while students supply responses; teachers decide on the length of an exchange, while students are cut off in the middle of their utterances. The teacher who decides on the order of other participants' turns is also the only possible addressee of any exchange initiated by another participant.

We language teachers and researchers would not be surprised to hear the following dialogue in an L2 classroom that is meant to teach learners a communicative use of the target language:

Teacher: David, ask Mary what her father's profession is.
Student B: (To Student C) Mary, what your father's profession is?
Teacher: No, say, what IS your father's profession.
Student B: What is your father's profession?
Teacher: Good.   (3.3)

In this segment, the teacher seems to be trying to help Student B create a short conversation with Student C. Unfortunately, this exchange does not appear to be a realistic dialogue between the two students due to the teacher's correction on Student B's grammar mistake ("No, say, what IS your father's profession?") and the teacher's follow-up feedback ("Good"). Apparently the original purpose of the exchange—to elicit information from Student C—has become to test if Student B can ask "WH" questions properly. L2 teachers often interrupt their students when they are supposed to hold a conversation with each other as this example suggests. Within this typical classroom interaction frame, L2 learners have limited opportunities to experience how real communication should be handled. The question is, whether learners can transfer knowledge learned in the classroom to real-life communication when classroom interaction reflects only a very small range of natural communication? Researchers and educators came to realize that classroom communication should more closely resemble communication outside the classroom.

WHAT DETERMINES "REAL" COMMUNICATION IN THE L2 CLASSROOM?

Our next question concerns what constitutes "genuine" communication in the L2 classroom. Before answering this question, we need to define the features that militate against real communication. The following dialogue, taken from Dinsmore (1985), provides an example from one so-called "communicative" language classroom. In this segment the teacher—a native speaker of English with EFL teaching experience in several countries—is role-playing a formal business interview with one of the students, a Japanese businessman with intermediate-level proficiency.

1 TA:		Fine. ok. right. mister Kato. I will interview you ok. ok so + fine. so + excuse me now. could you. could you please tell me ahm what your present job is?
2 S1:		I am a buyer and salesman
3 TA:		ah ha. I see. and ah. please can you give me your. ahm. full name
4 S1:		my name is Kazuhiro Kato
5 TA:		Kazuhiro Kato + h. how do you spell Kazuhiro Please
6 S1:		ahm K. A. Z. U. H. I. R. O.
7 TA:		uh huh I see. when were you born
8 S1:		I was born in six. in January. ah. six of January in 195. 54
9 TA:		ok. What's the preposition. I was born +
10 S1:		I was born in January
11 TA:		I was born in January. and what's the day
12 S1:		I was born in January sixth
13 TA:		ok look. wrong preposition
14 S1:		six
15 TA:		on
16 S1:		on + on. I was born on six + January. of January. six of January
17 TA:		ok on.
18 S1:		on + I was in the six.

(Data from Dinsmore, 1985)   (3.4)

Notice how awkwardly the teacher switches the conversational setting from the reality (present time, the classroom) to the pretended one (the office) in Turn 1, and how unnaturally the interview is carried on between the teacher and the student (e.g., "Kazuhiro Kato + h. how do you spell Kazuhiro please"). The teacher drops his mask and starts correcting the student's mistakes about using the proposition in Turn 9. The teacher also fully dominates the discourse topic from the beginning of the conversation. Dinsmore concludes that since the teacher, obviously, knows all the information about the student (his name and profession, for instance), the authenticity of the questions posed by the teacher in the interview is rather low and thus the communicative value of this role-play remains dubious.

British linguist and educator H. G. Widdowson defines the dual nature of language learning tasks in the classroom as learning the forms of the language and learning how to use them, or in his terms, the "usage" and "use" of the language (Widdowson, 1978). However, it seems to oversimplify the case if we attempt to describe classroom interactions from such a binary perspective as either focusing on "message" (thus, communication-oriented) or on "form" (grammar-oriented). Colyle and Bisgyer (1984) found a third language category called "restricted" language from their data collected from 15 language classrooms in the United States containing students with a variety of proficiency levels and ethnic backgrounds.

Restricted language is demonstrated in teacher's questions which appear in the interrogative form but carry the function of evaluating the students. For example,

   1. T: In the article, who helped Mrs. Johnson find her missing diamond?
           (Discussion question, text-based)   (3.5)

   2. T: What's the difference in connotation between "fat" and "chubby"?
           (Vocabulary building question)   (3.6)

   3. T: When is Christmas? (General truth question)   (3.7)

                     (examples taken from Coyle & Bisgyer, 1984)

These types of questions are meant to focus on the message (communication +), yet they involve no genuine transfer of information (communication −) for the teacher knows all the answers. "Unrestricted" language, on the contrary, contain genuine questions that aim to elicit information from the students that is unknown to the teacher.

Coyle and Bisgyer's (1984) analysis shows that in 8 out of the 15 classrooms observed, restricted questions outnumbered unrestricted, genuine ones. One of the major reasons that language teachers have not been able to move easily from the audiolingual approach into genuine communicative teaching, Coyle and Bisgyer suggest, is that these teachers are reverting to an approach termed "Mastery Questioning," which they experienced in their own elementary and secondary education. Student participation, according to the results of this study, is limited to responding to teacher solicitations. They find that the students, in general,

1.   seldom address questions to the teacher;
2.   almost never address questions to other students;
3.   almost never initiate new topics; and
4.   seldom react (ironically, it is the teacher who does most of the reacting in the class).

Coyle and Bisgyer suggest that in order to generate real communication in adult L2 classrooms, the following two conditions must be fulfilled:

1.   The language of the verbal interaction must be "unrestricted".
2.   In the pattern of discourse, the initiative must lie with the learners rather than with the teacher (Coyle & Bisgyer, 1984, p. 49).

Nunan (1987) reached a similar conclusion on teacher-student exchange patterns in a classroom-based study of communicative teaching. Nunan investigated the degree to which genuine communication is present in five supposedly communicative language lessons designed for

ESL students of mixed nationalities and language backgrounds. He found that even when teachers are committed to the concept of a communicative approach and all lessons focus on functional aspects of language use (e.g., elaborate jigsaw listening tasks, simulated interviews, and group discussion of magazine pictures in this study), the patterns of classroom interaction are identical to the basic I-R-F structure in mother-tongue classes. In other words, many language classes that are designed to promote communicative interactions may, in fact, not be as communicative as the teachers expected. Nunan suggests that "it is teachers themselves who need to become the *prime agents of change* through an increased sensitivity to what is really happening in their classes" (Nunan, 1987, p. 144, our italics).

Apparently, pseudo-communication occurs when the teacher and students do not have equal rights in speaking. In real-life conversations, people are usually symmetric in taking turns, selecting topics, and providing information within the topics agreed upon. It is also natural for participants in a conversation to assume their interlocutors follow these rules when conversing. If not, conversations may break down. It is reasonable to assume that if the teacher and students become as symmetric as people in real-life conversations, classroom interaction will have closer resemblance to everyday communication.

In order to examine the features of communicative versus non-communicative classroom discourse in greater detail, let us consider the characteristics of classroom interaction, both competitive and cooperative, described by Sjørslev (1987) (see Table 3.1). In a competitive interaction

TABLE 3.1.
Competitive versus Cooperative Classroom Interaction
Modified from Sjørslev's (1987) model

Interaction	Competitive	Cooperative
Turn taking	Turn taking rules are often violated. Many procedural problems occur.	Turn taking rules are usually followed. Few procedural problems occur.
Exchanges	Teachers frequently give directions; students never provide information.	Both teachers and students elicit information.
Amount of speech	Teachers take 2/3 or more; students take 1/3 or less. Students' contributions are short and contain mainly answering moves.	Teachers and students take around 1/2, respectively. Students' contributions are relatively long and contain both answering and opening moves.
Choice of topic and coherence	Only teacher-introduced topics are accepted as conversational topics. Topic coherence is established through the teacher's agenda for the lesson.	Both teacher- and student-introduced topics can be conversational topics. Topic coherence is established through negotiation between teachers and students.

relationship, the teacher is usually dominant in a conversation where the speech turns, exchanges, amounts of speech and topics are all under his/her control. In contrast, where a cooperative interaction relationship can be established in the classroom both the teacher and the students will make a similar contribution to the building of the conversation.

CONTINUUM OF CLASSROOM INTERACTION

Classroom interaction does not necessarily fall into the two extreme cases we discussed in the previous section (i.e., usage vs. use; form- vs. meaning-oriented; communication– vs. communication + ; asymmetric vs. symmetric). We view classroom interaction as a continuum between the two extremes. In Chapter One we proposed a continuum of drama approaches in language teaching. In fact, all pedagogical tasks can be characterized similarly according to the nature and quality of discourse they promote. Figure 3.1 illustrates a continuum of classroom interactions, proposed by Kramsch (1985), with natural discourse at one pole and instructional discourse at the other. Due to the different roles, tasks, and knowledge involved in pedagogical activities, classroom interaction moves freely along the continuum.

In an activity such as "teacher lecturing," the teacher and students usually have a fixed status, that is, authoritative speaker vs. passive receivers. The task to be performed for the teacher is delivering information to the class; the focus of interaction is on the accuracy of content-based knowledge to be delivered. In this case teacher-dominated talk and teacher-generated topics are likely to occur. Discourse generated in this type of activity falls on the "instructional" end on Kramsch's continuum. Activities containing more negotiable roles, promoting students participation, and emphasizing communication fluency over accuracy are more likely to create opportunities for

	Instructional discourse	Natural discourse
Role:	Fixed status	Negotiated roles
Tasks:	Teacher-oriented Position-centered	Group-oriented Person-centered
Knowledge:	Focus on content Accuracy of facts	Focus on process Fluency of interaction

FIGURE 3.1.   Continuum of classroom interaction
Source: Kramsch (1985).

the teacher and students to talk naturally and communicatively. Therefore more "natural" discourse will be generated in this type of classroom.

EXPLORING THE NATURE OF CLASSROOM DISCOURSE IN DRAMA ACTIVITIES

Problems in Classroom Research Into Second Language Acquisition Through Drama

Some language teachers have been using drama techniques for many years; others wait to be convinced of their utility. Those who use drama do so for a variety of reasons: new teaching ideas, a change of regular classroom activities, reducing learning anxiety, or simply having fun with students before the end of class bell rings. Interestingly, most literature that recommends drama approaches in language teaching is of an extremely practical nature (e.g., Anderson, 1989; Holden, 1981; Maley & Duff, 1978; Miller, 1986; Smith, 1984; Wright et al., 1980, to name just a few). Technical procedures for using different kinds of dramatic activities are described in detail in these publications but the rationales behind the pedagogical recommendations are mostly based on intuition or experience, rather than on empirical evidence.

One major reason for the scarcity of scientific research is that teacher-student interactions in drama activities appear to be more complex than those documented in many traditional pedagogical tasks. This complexity results from the fact that the teacher and students in drama activities "do attempt to break out of the constraints the classroom imposes as a social setting in terms of the types of talk that occur there" (Edmondson, 1985, p. 161). A drama-oriented language classroom is thus relatively more difficult to describe and investigate.

If curriculum designers claim that drama approaches create communicative environments in which learners may use the target language effectively, they must ground their claims in scientific analyses of the nature of classroom discourse. If language teachers intuitively claim that participating in drama activities enhances (or impedes) learning, they must also test their hypotheses by investigating the relationship between classroom instruction and the learning process. To sum up, in order to justify the utility of drama approaches in language teaching and learning, researchers and teachers must

1.   identify the significance of a particular drama approach in language learning;

2. explore what actually happens in classrooms when this approach is used;

3. find valid and reliable research instruments and measures to describe the event; and

4. be able to demonstrate that the relationships between this drama approach and student's learning outcomes are in some way causal (Modified from Ellis, 1990).

Four Studies of the Teacher's and Students' Language Use in Drama Activities

Several studies have been conducted on the impact of different kinds of drama on learners' verbal performance and teacher-student interaction in the classroom. Unfortunately, the majority of these studies are either researchers' descriptive analyses of their observations or comments on personal classroom experience without details about the data collection and analytical procedures (e.g., Anderson, 1989; Al-Khanji, 1987; Radin, 1985). It is difficult for other researchers and teachers to replicate studies of this kind with different groups of learners. This section discusses four particular studies that investigate the participants' interaction in drama. These four studies deserve our attention because in each of them the research design, data collection and analytical procedures have been scientifically explained by its researcher(s). Two of them were conducted in ESL settings and the other two investigated the use of drama in immersion classrooms.

Robert Di Pietro conducted a series of studies to discuss the utility and impact of "Strategic Interaction"—his particular pedagogical drama approach—on L2 learning and teaching (see Di Pietro, 1982, 1985, 1987a). His 1986 and 1987b studies are especially relevant to our discussion here. Subjects in both studies were beginning or intermediate-level students of various language backgrounds in the intensive ESL program at Delaware University. The students' verbal interactions during the "performance" stage in various scenarios were transcribed and analyzed.

Di Pietro's 1987 study investigated how L2 learners used different communication strategies to get their meaning across in various scenarios. Di Pietro analyzed the subjects' communication behavior based on Vygotsky's notion in which communication strategies are seen as efforts made by the speaker to achieve self-regulation in the presence of other speakers. Vygostsky (1978) proposed three types of regulations: object, other, and self. According to Vygotsky, an object-regulated speaker is one whose discourse is strongly constrained by the rules and conventions of the language in use. Other regulation is of two types: discourse regulated by others and regulating others. In the former type one's verbal performance is directed by another person. The latter type describes the same phenomenon but from the other individual's point of departure. Self-regulation occurs when one speaker feels free to express personal thoughts, positions or feelings. Examples of object-regulated discourse in L2 classroom are the utterances of learners while performing grammatical drills or routine exercises— their discourse are fully restricted by the rules or language patterns of the activities. Other-regulation discourse is similar to conversations that follow the typical I-R-F structure in which the teacher often directs the discourse through restricted questions. Self-regulation—an important characteristic in natural discourse—occurs when the speaker is asked to speak freely on a subject. Di Pietro pointed out that a characteristic of authentic discourse in real-life situations is that object-, other- and, particularly, self-regulation are used alternately in communication.

The following conversation between two learners in one of the scenarios shows how messages are exchanged in a strategic interaction. The dialogue takes place on a train between a traveling salesperson who deals with clothes (Role A) and a passenger in the next seat (Role B). A tries to make a business conversation with B who believes A is somebody who once sold an expensive but defective TV to him.

A:	Where are you going?
B:	Oh, I going to New York City (How about you?)
A:	First, good, I have to pass in. in the New New York because I. I just returned to the country. You are pretty today! Where you buy your clothes?
B:	Let me. let me. oh I remember that uhhh me meet..in another time.
A:	Oh, I don't think.
B:	Oh yes! You sold me a (TV) a television set in a...once...time.
A:	No... I don't think so
B:	(you) you remember in the last year...more or less in July...I went to the...uhh...Radio Shack store...you work-ed there?
A:	Minute, please, just a minute.
	(A goes to her group for consultation and then returns to the scene)
A:	Sir, I think you're wrong because I . my job is
B:	I am sure
A:	No, no
B:	because
A:	You you make a mistake you make a mistake because I, I'm traveling sales . sales . only sport
Teacher:	clothing
A:	Huh?
Teacher:	clothing.
A:	only sales clothing...OK? I think you're you're...y you're you're you're

B: I am sure because uh . uh . for your bad sold . I lost so
                much...money.

A: No, no...you're crazy . you are crazy...you are very crazy.

                                            (Data from Di Pietro, 1987, p. 10)   (3.7)

In this short segment of conversation, B is clearly on the offensive side
in trying to have A admit to being engaged in an earlier transaction with
him. A also counterattacks by telling B that B "makes a mistake" and is
"crazy." A tries to clarify that she sells clothes but not electrical appliances.
Although both learners have some difficulties in pronunciation, grammar,
and vocabulary and therefore repeat themselves frequently (i.e., object-
regulation discourse occurs), their primary intention is to fulfill their individual goals in the conversation. Results of this study show that all the three
types of discourse regulation are used by the learners in their verbal
exchanges in strategic interaction activities. More importantly, the domi-
nating agency of learner's discourse is self-regulation; scenarios, thus, stimulate L2 learners to engage in self-regulation in the interaction.

Di Pietro's 1986 study examined the contribution of participating in scenarios to the acquisition of the target language. A careful comparison is
made between the students' initial verbal performance in scenarios and
their second performance of the same themes after receiving some support and advice from the teacher. Remarkable differences are found in the
use of "communicative strategies" and in control of vocabulary and mechanisms. Communicative strategies are used by L2 learners (and native speakers) when they are faced by a production problem. These include
reduction strategies, which are used to avoid problem (e.g., to reduce or
simplify uncertain elements in conversation) and achievement strategies,
which are used to overcome problem (e.g., to use exaggerating intonation
or body language to help the expression).

Di Pietro found that the subjects used more communicative strategies,
such as hesitation, repair, repetition, counter question, and body language
in their first performance because at that point they had less control of the
vocabulary and mechanisms. The subjects used fewer communicative strategies as they became more confident with the target language in their second performance. The increased confidence together with the built-in
interactive tension in scenarios induced the participants to try alternative
more sophisticated approaches in achieving their individual goals in the
second performance of the same scenario. Di Pietro explained that the
planning allowed by the rehearsal phase, appropriate assistance from the
teacher during the two performances, and the internal tension carried by
the activity contributed most to the progress of the learners' competence
in communication.

Wilburn's study of 1992 is the third to be discussed. This study was a part of a research project that investigates language teaching and learning in immersion schools in America (see Bernhardt, 1992). One major aim of Wilburn's ethnographic study was to understand how the inclusion of drama affects classroom discourse in an immersion setting. Records of the classroom activities and the researcher's field notes were collected over an eight-month period from three elementary classes of different grades in a Spanish immersion school in the midwestern United States.

The most interesting finding regarding classroom discourse is that the participants' language produced in drama tends to be more authentic and native-like than that evoked by traditional tasks. One may argue that immersion settings are already meaningful contexts for speaking; consequently, learners' language must be authentic. Ironically, many studies about the language use of immersion students show that classroom dialect or pidgin characterizes the speech (e.g., Green & Harker, 1988). In other words, immersion students' language can be very fluent but may often lack authenticity. This unsatisfactory learning outcome may be largely the result of the teachers' didactic language style and the use of "display questions"— questions to which the students already know the answers.

Wilburn looked at the characteristics of immersion students' discourse in process drama activities. Although the influence of the students' native language was identifiable, the syntactical structure and style of their language was generally more natural than in traditional tasks. Interestingly, the teacher's style of speaking in the drama was also different from the more dominant tone apparent in many regular classroom activities. The following dialogue taken from Wilburn's data provides a vivid picture of how the teacher and the students used the target language naturally. The drama is based on a popular children's picture book *Where the Wild Things Are*, written by Maurice Sendak (1963). A telephone conversation is carried on by Max's mother (the teacher in role T) and a policeman (one of the first-grade students in role S). An English translation provided by Wilburn follows the dialogue.

S: La mamá de Max. La mamá de Max. Hello, Hello. Max está en un danger zone.

T: Y ¿Por qué? ¿Qué le Pasó?

S: Le...Se...A Hora no puede leer. (Sign was in English, not in Spanish.)

T: ¿No puede leer?

S: Sí. Y se va a una cave. Con los osos.

T: ¿A una cueva? ¿Y los osos se lo van a comer? Le dió. Le dió. ¿Le hizo así? (makes slapping gesture) Pero, Max está vivo o está meurto?

S: Está...¿cómo se dice 'hurt'?

T: Oh. ¿está hurido?

S: Sí, está mucho adido.

T: Y por qué tú no lo sacas de la cueva, policía?

S: Porque mira la mapa. Porque tiene que...

T: ¿Cómo qué no puedes hacer nada? Mi hijo está en la cueva con los osos y tú está a quí? Por qué tú no tienes los policía en esa cueva ahora mismo? ¡Andale! Ve a poner los policía y tráeme a Max.

S: Sí. Adiós.

T: Adiós.

> [S: Max's mom. Max's mom. Hello, Hello. Max is in a danger zone. T: Why? What happened? S: He can't read now. (Sign was in English and Max only reads Spanish.) T: He can't read? S: Right. And he went into a cave. With bears. T: In a cave? And the bears are going to eat him? And they're slapping him around? But... is Max dead or alive? S: He's...how do you say 'hurt'? T: Oh. He is hurt. S: Yes, he's hurt (intended) a lot. T: Why aren't the police getting him out of the cave? S: because they're looking at a map. They need to...T: How can you do nothing? My son is in a cave with bears and you're here. Why don't you have the police in the cave right now? Get going. Call in the police and bring me to Max. S: Yes (Ma'am) goodbye. T: Goodbye.]

> (data taken from Wilburn, 1992; the English translation is Wilburn's)
>
> (3.8)

Wilburn points out that teachers speak very differently in drama from the way they usually speak in traditional classroom activities because they must switch to a more dialectic format when they are in role. She also suggests that the teacher's function changes from a message deliverer to an information sharer in this example because they are a part of the situation. Students' language is also found to be different from that produced in a traditional activity because students are responsible for making themselves understood and for making meaning from others' utterances in order to participate in drama built up by the whole class. The most interesting phenomenon found in this study is that these elementary school students are able to extend their word choices, language functions, registers, and stylistics in drama, which makes their language use more authentic and communication-oriented.

The final study to be discussed is a teacher-researcher study conducted by three elementary school teachers investigating language interactions in their own French immersion classrooms (Shacker et al., 1993). This study explores the implementation and frequency of occurrences of four language functions, namely, *informative, directive, expressive,* and *imaginative* (*Le français à l'élémentaire,* 1987), in group drama. Students' verbal interactions in 12 drama sessions were first transcribed from the video- and audio-records and then analyzed according to a coding system.

Their definitions of the four language functions are summarized as follows:

1. Informative: to obtain or give information, for example, Quoi est des pelles? (What are shovels?)
2. Directive: to request help, give permissions, or make commands, for example, "Venez avec moi, vite!" (Come with me, quick(ly)).
3. Expressive: to express personal feelings, opinions or ideas, for example, "J'ai mal à la doigt" (I had a sore finger).
4. Imaginative: for diversion, entertainment, or stimulation of the imagination, for example, "J'ai cinquante sous, maman" (I have 50 cents, mom)—the speaker changes the tone to very childish as to define the role in drama.

Their analysis shows that the informative function occurs in all group drama sessions with a high frequency. This function is used when children intend to inform others, ask for information from others, or acquire new information. The occurrence rate of directive language is low across all sessions. However, this function appears more frequently in task-oriented activities and less frequently during the oral discussion or problem solving sessions. Interestingly, students are able to distinguish the subtle differences between different types of directive language. They make gentle requests when having tasks to perform and give blunt commands when time is of the essence and actions are fast paced.

Expressive language occurs most frequently in reflection and problem solving sessions. These two types of activities provide most opportunities for the students to use the expressive function in meaningful communication. The imaginative language function is used in all sessions during the group drama. Students tend to use this function to create a dramatic climax and authentic atmosphere in the classroom. Shacker and associates (1993) suggest that different focuses of group drama sessions, particularly those containing problem solving and student-directed tasks, provide language learners with a wide range of contexts in which the four functions naturally occur in oral communication.

All four studies have examined the nature of learner discourse. One looked at the teacher's use of language (Wilburn, 1992), and two investigated the relations between the nature of drama activities and learners' performance (Di Pietro, 1986; Shacker et al., 1993). However, some questions regarding teacher-student interaction remain unanswered in their discussions.

The data in Di Pietro's two studies were collected during the performance phase of scenarios. During this phase, although the conversation is usually carried between two particular participants, they can stop the scene when they get stuck and ask for help from their group members. Di Pietro did not discuss how other students' help from outside the scene may have influenced the participants' performance during this phase. Furthermore, it is not clear how the students' second performance might change if there were no assistance from the teacher between the two phases. Shacker and associates do examine how a group of learners (19 students, in their study) use language differently in situations with or without the teacher's presence. Unfortunately, because the teacher's contribution is not their research interest, they devote little discussion to the function of the teacher talk in the interaction.

Wilburn is the only researcher who touches on the issue of teacher-student interaction in her analysis, with several short segments of teacher-student verbal exchanges. However, her descriptive analysis does not give a complete picture of what is happening between the teacher and learners in drama. Since all the four studies acknowledge that drama creates authentic conversational situations, a more extensive analysis of how discourse exchanges are initiated and managed in drama is necessary.

Characteristics of Classroom Interaction: Turn Taking and Participants' Initiative

Sociolinguist Leo van Lier's notion of classroom interaction provides a comprehensive starting point for conducting research into the nature of teacher-student interaction (see van Lier 1984b; 1988). According to van Lier, the most critical feature while analyzing classroom discourse is to examine how speakers take turns in a conversation, because turn taking reveals the level of individual speaker's involvement in the interaction. He suggests that the equal-rights status of natural conversation creates some rules accepted by participants in a conversation. For example, the current speaker may select the next speaker, and the next speaker may decide to speak when certain signals are given by the current speaker to indicate his willingness to yield the floor. Once the commonly accepted rules are violated, the conversation may be broken or carried on under an asymmetric condition.

The teacher-students interactional relationship observed by Sinclair and Coulthard provides a good example of how conversations are carried on in an asymmetric manner. In our Dialogue 3.1, the teacher first decides who will speak next by summoning one particular student and then immediately takes back the floor by commenting on this speaker's utterances and nominating the speaker of the next turn. The other participants, the students, seem to take the teacher's superiority for granted and support the conversation in a very cooperative manner. This conversation appears to flow smoothly but it is clearly dominated by one particular participant who controls how speech turns should be taken. Interaction of this kind happens not only in school contexts but in many other situations where certain speakers have more power, socially or professionally, than the others, such as a conversation between an employer and employees in a formal company meeting. However, a more even distribution of turn-control among all participants is usually expected in casual conversations.

Examining the distribution of speech turns in a conversation allows researchers to understand how the interaction is built up, as well as clarifying each speaker's role within the interaction. A carefully defined classification is needed for this kind of analysis. The central goal of constructing such a classification is to identify participants' "initiative." Initiative is recognized when speakers select or allocate a turn. It is important for the researcher to distinguish whether a particular student's contribution is initiated by him/herself or is mainly a response to the teacher's utterance. Initiative is also reflected in the ways one topic is maintained and/or shifted from one to another during the exchanges. For example, switching the current topic to something else means having control in the conversation, but talking about topics established by previous speakers is mainly to support and to maintain the interaction.

Initiative, therefore, can be interpreted in any of the following four ways:

A.   Topic management: The current turn introduces something new or denies a request of a prior trn.
B.   Self-selection: One speaker decides to speak without being forced.
C.   Allocation: The current speaker appoints the speaker of the next turn, content to be talked about, or activity to be performed.
D.   Sequencing activity or discourse: The current turn is the opening or closing part of a sequence of turns.

Many classroom interaction studies postulate that the equal-rights status of real-life communication is suspended in traditional classroom activities. The teacher is the supreme ruler who appoints a certain student (or a group of students) as the next speaker(s) and takes the turn back after the appointed speaker(s) responds to the call. Topic control also becomes the exclusive territory of the teacher in the classroom. Since we claim that the teacher-student interaction in drama activities resembles real-life communication, it is necessary to investigate how the teacher and students manage their turns differently from what we have observed in many traditional classroom situations. van Lier's notions of turn taking and turn initiative are based on the way people communicate in real situations are particularly useful analytical tools to compare the nature of teacher-student interaction with real-life conversation.

A STUDY OF TEACHER-STUDENT INTERACTION IN PROCESS DRAMA ACTIVITIES

A drama-oriented language classroom is a place where knowledge is transmitted through the process of unfolding dramatic situations. Studies of the impact of drama on language learning should thus shift the attention from examining the learner's or teacher's individual discourse to analyzing the interaction among all parties. Spoelder's remarks (1987) of the problematic nature of classroom studies reflect our concerns about research into drama activities:

> Today, the thesis "education is communication" can no longer be defended without taking into account the developments and research generated in some disciplines. The focus is no longer on either the sender or the receiver, but rather on the mechanics of educational discourse, its constraints, aims and functions in a larger context. (p. 205)

In this section we will discuss a teacher-researcher study conducted by Kao (1994), which views classroom activities as a process developed by the teacher and the students together. The focus of this study is placed neither on teaching nor learning, but on the nature of interaction and its impact on learning as well as teaching. The objectives of this study were to

1. describe the nature of teacher-student participation patterns;
2. examine the impact of different drama themes on participants' performance;
3. understand the relationship between the learners' drama experience and the growth of their communicative competence; and
4. provide evidence for the claim that the classroom context created in process drama is close to natural situations and thus powerful in activating the learners' linguistic knowledge and developing their spontaneity in communication.

Background to the Study and the Participants

This study took place in a drama-oriented English course for regular first-year university students in National Cheng Kung University, Tainan, Taiwan in the first semester of the 1992–1993 school year. The 33 students enrolling in this course were from the School of Engineering or Science in this university. Generally, students who are admitted to any university in Taiwan have studied English as a compulsory subject for six years in high school and have passed a highly competitive national examination, the Joint College Entrance Examination (JCEE),[1] in which English is a major testing subject. According to the annual report of the Board of JCEE in 1992, the mean English test score of the upper 50 percent of all examination takers was 54 out of 100 and the mean score for all examinees was 37 for that year. The mean score of the students of this study, 54.41, was very close to that of the upper 50 percent of the examinees for that year. Clearly, the students in this study possessed a certain degree of linguistic knowledge.

To understand the students' prior experience of studying English in high school, a questionnaire was administered to the class (see Appendix A for the questionnaire). Information gathered includes their English scores on the entrance examination, types of instruction they received in high school English classes, and self-evaluation of their English proficiency (see Appendix B for the summary of the students' responses to the questionnaire). It was found that about 80 percent of the 33 students had received reading, writing and grammar instruction in high school, but only about 30 percent of the class had received instruction in speaking and/or listening (see Table 3.2). The instructional patterns indicate that the primary educational interest in Taiwanese high school English classrooms is to prepare the students for passing the English test on JCEE and not to teach them how to use the language for real communication.

TABLE 3.2.
Frequency and Percentage of Five Instructional Emphasis at High School Level for All Subjects

Instructional Emphasis	Frequency	Percentage
Listening		
No	23	69.7
Yes	10	30.3
Speaking		
No	22	66.7
Yes	11	33.3
Reading		
No	4	12.1
Yes	29	87.9
Writing		
No	8	24.2
Yes	25	75.8
Grammar		
No	6	18.2
Yes	27	81.8

Note: $N = 33$.

Classroom activities were designed according to two approaches, realistic and imaginary, in order to investigate the influence of different themes on participants' oral performance. Audio- and video-records were taken in every class meeting throughout the course and the researcher's up-to-date field notes were kept immediately after each class. Records of four complete drama sessions—using two realistic and two imaginary themes—were then randomly selected from the data pool for detailed analysis.

Task based pre- and post-course oral proficiency tests were given to the students to determine at what level the students started and ended in the course. The task was to describe a cartoon-strip story—containing some pictures—to a listener who did not know the story and needed to identify the sequence of scenes (see pp. 73–4 for the pictures used in the two tests). The task creates situations in which the speaker has to produce extended speech for communication. The pre- and post-tests elicited valuable information about the growth of individual students' communicative competence during the period of the study.

The Coding System and Analytical Procedures for Classroom Interaction Analysis

The coding system used for classroom interaction analysis was originally developed by van Lier (1988) based on the notion of turn taking and turn initiative in communication. Raw data were first transcribed, based on turns exchanged between speakers. Each turn or turn part was then classified according to its initiative elements. As van Lier has identified, initiative in communication can be shown in four ways:

A. topic management;
B. self-selection;
C. allocation; and
D. sequencing.

A turn or turn part was given a mark if its nature was consistent with any of the four categories described in this coding system. Therefore, a turn may receive more than one star. Three independent raters were invited to score the data for this study. Two training sessions had been given to the raters before the final scores were made. Any confusion about the classification and disagreements in scores were discussed during the training sessions. Dialogue 3.9, a short exchange between two students and the teacher, taken from one of the four activities in this study, illustrates how the data were coded by one of the raters using this system. In this segment the three participants were talking about how Frank—a male student who took on a role as an environmentalist—gathered information about Taiwanese businessmen stockpiling rhino horns.

Initiative Categories				Turn	Speaker	Speech
A	B	C	D			
	*	*	* 64		T	e:h you got the figures from..the local..eh:: manufacturer in Africa?
*			* 65		Frank	no..it was from the local man..and I pretend that I am a manufacturer in Taiwan...so that is=
		*	66		T	[o::h..
					Frank	true...
*	*	*	* 67		T	this person, this Dr. Frank.. pretend.. he is a...manufacturer...in Taiwan...=
	2*		68–9		Frank	[ye:ah.. [ye:ah
					T	=so you cheated...
		*	* 70		Frank	yes: of course...there are many...
	*	*	* 71		T	so you pretend you are a manufacturer from Taiwan and told the people in Africa that you want to buy rhino horns for Taiwan...
			* 72		Frank	yes
*	*	*	* 73		CS	so you just guess!
			* 74		Frank	no, no, I not guess!
*	*	*	* 75		CS	you don't have the true information.. .
			* 76		Frank	yes... the information is true.. .
*	*	*	* 77		CS	where is the information?
*			* 78		Frank	the information.. I told you!..that there are ten tons of rhino horns..

(3.9)

The total number of turns and the total number of marks of individual participants were then computed. The total number of turns Speaker X contributes to the entire activity is called the Quantity Index of X's participation. Due to the fact that the length of activities varied, Speaker X's total number of speech turns was transformed into percentage turn for the convenience of cross-activity comparison. Therefore,

$$\text{Speaker X's total turn percentage (TT\%)} = \frac{\text{Speaker X's total number of turns}}{\text{Total number of turns made by the class}}$$

Formula 3.1. Individual Speaker's Total Turn Percentage

The total number of marks Speaker X obtained is called the Participation Value (PV). It is the Quality Index of Speaker X's participation. Accordingly, we introduce

$$\text{Speaker X's participation level (PL)} = \frac{\text{Speaker X's Participation Value}}{\text{Speaker X's total number of turns}} = \frac{\text{PV}}{\text{TT}}$$

Formula 3.2. Individual Speaker's Participation Level

In order to take into account both the quantity and the quality of Speaker X's verbal contribution in the later analysis, the following concept is used as the participation index (PI) for Speaker X:

$$PI = (PL)^2 \, (TT\%)$$

Formula 3.3. Individual Speaker's Participation Index

The total percentage of the agreement among the three raters is 85.4 percent. A special computational model and a computer program were developed to calculate the "master score" from the three raters' judgments for the analysis. The percentage of agreement between each rater and the master score was calculated—the percentage of agreement ranged from 90 percent to 96 percent. A "weight" was given to each rater's score according this agreement percentage and a master scoretable was constructed. The advantage of constructing the master scoretable is to take all rates' opinions into account according to their reliability. The results obtained from this procedure are more accurate than those obtained from "majority voting" or "averaging out" (see Kao, 1994, for the details of this procedure).

The Analytical Procedures for the Oral Proficiency Tests

The students' verbal protocols in the oral tests were scored in two respects: the clarity of the account and the number of communication units (CU) the account contained. A scoring matrix was developed to evaluate the clarity of the students' speech. Two independent raters were invited to score the data obtained from the two tests. The percentage of agreement between the two raters was 90 percent. We then took an average from the scores given by the two raters for later discussion and statistical analysis.

The Four Activities

The entire study proceeded during a 14-week-long period. For the purpose of data analysis, four activities—two with imaginative and two with realistic themes—were randomly selected from the data pool for detailed analysis of the participants' interaction patterns. Brief descriptions of the procedures and the background stories of the four activities follow.

1. Activity 1—B. B. Wolf

This activity was loosely based on the story of "The Three Little Pigs and the Big Bad Wolf." The class had reviewed the original story prior to the activity. At the beginning of this session, the teacher told the class that the "Big Bad Wolf" claimed that he had been badly burned due to the trick the third pig had played on him and he had decided to sue the pigs. The class was divided into two groups. One group took the role of police officers who were sent to interview the forest animals, played by the students in the second group, to investigate what happened when the wolf "visited" the pigs. After this short pair-work, a trial was held in which the police and the animals were invited to give their testimonies about the case. The teacher was in role as the judge in the court. After listening to the police officers' reports and the testimonies of the animals, the class formed a jury to discuss the case. The jury decided the pigs were not guilty regarding the wolf's injury, but the wolf was responsible for the pigs' property loss. The wolf was required to rebuild the house for the pigs as his punishment. The activity discussed in this study was the entire trial, which took about 30 minutes.

2. Activity 2—Martial Law

This activity was based on *Tuesday*, a children's picture book written by Wiesner (1991). In the first session, a situation was created in which the residents of Pond City (an imaginative place) found thousands of water lily leaves scattered all over the city one Wednesday morning. A police investigation was carried out. Many people claimed they had heard unusual sounds and witnessed strange flying objects in the night. Some others believed there was a scientific experiment going on near their town. No specific conclusion was drawn at the end of this first session. At the beginning of the second session—the activity discussed in this study—the teacher took the role of an army general telling the townspeople that martial law would be announced in 24 hours because the security of the town was in doubt. A citizen's meeting was then called to discuss the matter. A heated debate arose between those who agreed with the imposition of martial law and those who opposed it. This activity took about 25 minutes.

3. Activity 3—Rhino Horns

This topic was a realistic issue in which two international environmental groups accused Taiwanese businessman of stockpiling rhino horns. The students were divided into small groups representing the two environmental groups, government officials of Taiwan, the Chinese Medicine Association, and university professors. They were all invited to give their opinion in a TV documentary program hosted by the teacher. This activity took about 35 minutes.

4. Activity 4—Salesmen

The last activity was also based on a realistic topic. The class was randomly divided into two groups. Members of one group became door-to-door salesmen and students of the other group were residents of a small community. The salesmen had 10 minutes to persuade their potential customers to buy their products. After this pair activity, two short group meetings were held. One was a meeting of residents to discuss the problem of annoying salesmen trying to sell goods in their neighborhood and the other was a discussion of strategies among the salesmen for selling more products to make a better profit for their company. Each of the meetings took about 12 minutes. We analyze the two group meetings in the study.

A Descriptive Discourse Analysis

Analyzing the transcriptions from a descriptive approach is the most direct way to obtain information about the way these participants interacted in the drama activities. Results of previous studies of classroom discourse in drama have pointed out that the teacher-student interaction pattern is more complex and the use of the target language more authentic than that found in traditional classroom tasks (e.g., Di Pietro, 1987b; Wilburn, 1992). Similar features were also noticed in the participants' verbal performance in this study. The students' verbal performance appeared more fluent and meaning-oriented in drama than that produced when they were not in role. It was also noticed that the students were very much involved in shaping the scenes and therefore possessed a certain control over the direction of the conversation as the drama unfolded. Various strategies to control the progress of the situation were detected in the students' utterances.

To explore these characteristics of the participants' verbal performance in drama further, let us review the conversation in Dialogue 3.10 as an example. This segment is taken from Turns 82 to 161 of Activity 2—Martial Law—of the study, in which the citizens of Pond City were debating whether they needed martial law. The general (the teacher) and her two assistant officers (voluntary students, Francis and Kevin) had been ordered by their superior officer to convince the residents of the city that implementing this law was for the sake of the people's own safety. However, many residents disagreed with the conditions of martial law which restricted walking on the street after the sunset, running a business in the night, discussing this mysterious event in public, and traveling outside the city without special permission until the investigation was completed.

Turn	Speaker	Speech
82	Sunny	we don't have any income, and what should we do during this time:..
83	Francis	you can go out in the day time, okay? you can do the normal things in the day time, okay? you just, just stay home at the night..
84	Sunny	but some people, like piano pub will open in the night..
85	T	piano pub? that's not a good business..=
86	LL	((laughing))
	T	=from my point of view, you shouldn't go to the piano bar, even without the martial law, right?
87	LL	((laughing))
88	T	are you the owner of the piano bar? (to Sunny)
89	Sunny	((laughing, shaking her head))
90	T	then what kind of business are you doing...
91	L	begger !
92	L	from outer space!
93	LL	((laughing)) ((unint))
94	Sunny	I am a student!
95	T	you are a student! so it's none of your business, either =
96	LL	((laughing))
97	T	Okay:, if those people, those owners: of the piano bars, don't object to it, it's none of your business then!
98	CS	((raising his hand))
99	Francis	one more there ((point to CS))
100	T	okay
101	CS	I don't like the martial law very much!
102	T	how dare you!
103	LL	((laughing))
104	CS	because it, it affect my life very much.. it affect my freedom...
105	T	your freedom!
106	CS	yes! in fact, at that night, nobody get hurt.
107	T	nobody got hurt?
108	CS	yes:
109	T	that's your luck:. I mean, this week you don't get hurt, but next week, probably, you will:.
110	CS	((smiling)) but, but we know, that really nobody got hur:t..
111	T	we are not very sure about that...
112	CS	but I don't like it..
113	T	you don't like what?
114	CS	the martial law...
115	Francis	but we don't like it either, but we must wor:k..
116	T	yes, we don't like it either, we got extra work! I have to stay up, usually I go to bed early, because of this work I have to be awake, but we are here to protect you..

117	Francis	ye:s..
118	LL	((laughing))
119	T	we don't like it either, really, I have to tell you
120	Jason	((raising his hand))
121	T	it's you again!
122	LL	((laughing))
123	Jason	I hate this martial law, and now, I want to move out the city.. can I?
124	T	you have the freedom, you can go... =
125	LL	((laughing))
	T	= this martial law is really for a short time, okay, after the police: headquarter finds out the truth, there won't be any martial law...
126	Jason	but in the, in this period of time, wha:t, what..
127	T	if you want o move out, move ! ((point to the door))
128	LL	((laughing))
129	Jason	that, that's the question, okay, I don't know what are you, what are the government doing..during this period of time..
130	T	you mean, you mean what the government will do =
131	Jason	eh:ee:
	T	= during the time when the martial law is effective...
132	Francis	we will investigate..
133	T	yes, we will investigate.. =
134	LL	((unint))
	T	=investigate means doing what.. what's investigate..
135	Kevin	調查 (=investigate)
136	T	okay:.. we will investigate this , this case..
137	Jason	((laughing))
138	T	are you satisfied? we are here to help you... ladies and gentlemen..
139	Dick	((raising his hand))
140	T	okay
141	Dick	can you give me the finish time of this la:w.. if you cannot find out the truth forever, we should obey the law for:ever..
142	F&K	((unint)) ((looking at each other and then discuss between themselves softly))
143	Francis	I think we will, we will do this matter in a:, a month time:.. if we cannot get any answer, we will leave!
144	Kevin	ye:s
145	Francis	yes, one month
146	T	okay, General Francisco said one month, are you satisfied?
147	L	no!
148	T	okay, somebody say no! if you don't agree with this martial law, you must speak out.. after today, you won't have any chance...

149	Collins	((raising his hand))
150	T	who is that gentleman?.. are you.. are you the mayor?
151	Collins	((unint)) ye::s ((very softly))
152	T	are you the mayor?
153	Collins	yes! ((louder))
154	T	o:h, you are the mayor.. what do you want to say, mayor!
155	Collins	((smiling)) I think, first, I don't think you can do something during the time..
156	Francis	why
157	Collins	okay, second, I want to ask everybody here, who wants the law... y:es...
158	T	s:o you want a vote..
159	Collins	((smiling)) e:h.. ask everybody..
160	T	e:ah..
161	Collins	yes, and ask everybody here, who wants the government to do this...

(3.10)

In her utterances, Sunny (a female student), expressed her concerns about how Martial Law might affect people's daily lives and business. In Turns 82 and 84 Sunny asked the military officers how people were supposed to make a living if they could not do their business at night. Francis, in Turn 83, avoided giving a direct answer but provided her with some alternatives. The teacher, similarly, switched attention away from the issue by commenting that running piano bars is "not a good business." In Turn 101, CS, a male student, tried to use a much more direct way to reopen the topic of the inconvenience martial law would cause to the people. In Turns 104, 106, 110, and 112 he frankly stated his dislike of these conditions in a very strong tone—"I don't like it" and "it affects my freedom." Furthermore, CS argued that martial law was unnecessary since "nobody got hurt at that night" (Turns 106 and 110).

Jason, a male student who had previously expressed his opposition against martial law in question form, (not shown in this dialogue) stood up and threatened to move out of the city if the law was enforced (Turn 123). However, his strategy did not achieve his goal. On the contrary, the general replied to him, saying: "you have the freedom, you can go . . ." (Turn 124). This student immediately realized that posing threats would not work, so he changed his topic to what the government would do to improve conditions in Turns 126 and 129. This time he received a more direct response from one of the military men—"we'll investigate" (Francis, Turn 132). Dick, another male student, took this opportunity to ask the military officers to determine a definite time to end martial law in Turn 141.

The drama seemed to have reached its end at the moment that the cessation of martial law was promised by the two assistant generals, Francis and Kevin. Surprisingly, Collins, a male student, stood up from the back of the classroom claiming to be the mayor of the city and asking for a citizen vote on the issue. Obviously, this student realized that the majority of the class disagreed with the imposition of martial law so there would be a better chance for them to win the case unconditionally if it could be settled in a public vote. The drama thus swiftly changed to a new direction that no participant (not even the teacher) could have anticipated.

It is also interesting to note how the assistant officers, played by two students, reacted to the challenges initiated by their peers in role. Francis and Kevin did not hesitate while facing their classmates' sharp questions. On the contrary, they skillfully made use of their superior status and properly exercised the power they had been given when speaking to their classmates.

It is amazing how fluently these students used the target language for communication. Among the 79 exchanges in this segment, the conversation was stopped only once due to unfamiliar vocabulary (from Turns 133 to 135) when the teacher and Kevin explained to the class what "investigate" meant. Otherwise, communication went on smoothly and all language problems (or misunderstandings) were clarified within the drama by repeating, posing questions, trying alternative expressions and other techniques of "repair" in a rather indirect manner. For example, in Turn 129, Jason's question was grammatically incorrect and its meaning was not very clear either: "I don't know what are you, what are the government doing . . . during this period of time." The teacher then repeated the question in the correct form and meanwhile clarified the meaning to the class in Turn 130: " you mean what the government will do during . . during the time when the martial law is effective." The next speaker, Francis, picked up the form quickly by replying that "we *will* investigate" (Turn 132).

Compared with their fluency, the accuracy of the students' language usage does not appear to be that impressive. There are noticeable problems in their word choices, sentence structures, and grammar. For example, in Turn 141 Dick said "can you give me the *finish time* of the law . . . if you cannot find out the truth forever, *we should* obey the law forever." "Finish time" is not an appropriate word choice which is probably a direct translation from the learner's mother tongue—Chinese. What this learner meant here is the "ending date" of the martial law. The second sentence in this turn is incorrect in its structure. It should be a question: Should we obey the law forever, if you never find out the truth? Examples of these types are not rare in this group of learners' conversation in the drama activities. Interestingly, the inappropriate language use did not seem to affect the proceeding of the drama too much. One possible explanation is that with sufficient understanding about the theme and the content of other speakers' utterances, a participant can still take part in the drama even when other speakers do not speak perfectly. This is quite similar to our experience in real-life conversation. Participants in natural communication seldom stop their interlocutors for incorrect sentence structures or language usage, unless the meaning of the utterances become ambiguous and the understanding is affected. This is because natural conversation is meaning-oriented. Conversation in process drama activities carries this "fluency over accuracy" feature too.

The advantage arising from this feature is that the drama proceeds without artificial interruptions. However, to help the students progress to a more advanced level in their linguistic competence is still a goal in every L2 language program and it will be necessary to help the students improve the accuracy of their language within and beyond the drama. In chapter 5 we discuss in more detail ways of achieving this educational goal through the careful structuring of a drama-oriented course.

Descriptive analysis is useful in providing details of the complex patterns in which the turns and discourse topics are managed among the participants. However, this type of analysis is not appropriate for comparing interactions among different speakers across several activities. It is necessary to examine the data with more systematic procedures. The following sections present the results of our analysis of the four drama activities with the notion of initiative proposed by van Lier (1988).

The Quantity and Quality of the Teacher's Versus Students' Discourse Across the Four Activities

The number of turns a speaker takes in a conversation is, as we mentioned earlier, the quantity index of this person's speech. In order to understand the distribution of speech turns contributed by the teacher and students across the four drama activities discussed earlier, a comparison was made in terms of the percentage of turns produced by these two parties (see Figure 3.2). Clearly, the students together took almost 20 percent more turns than the teacher across the four activities. This pattern indicates that the students together generally spoke more often than the teacher.

The differences between these two groups in terms of their participation quality (in other words, the participation value either group obtained) were not as obvious as those found in the comparison of their participation quantity (see Figure 3.3). The students and the teacher gave almost equally valuable verbal contributions in Activity 1—B.B. Wolf, Activity 2—Martial Law, and Activity 3—Rhino Horns. However, there was a greater difference between these two groups in Activity 4—Salesman, where the teacher contributed about 20 percent higher participation value—in terms of speech effectiveness—than all the students combined. This great difference between students and teacher may have been caused by the different format of the activities. Activity 4 consisted of two distinct segments with half of the class speaking in each, while the other three activities involved the

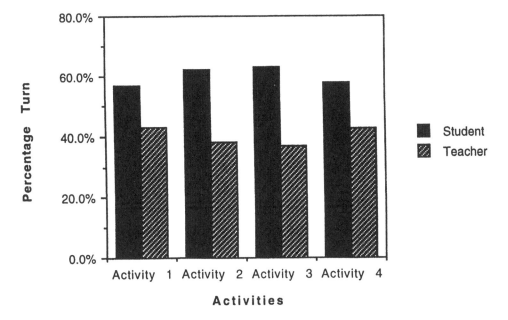

FIGURE 3.2.   Percentage of students' versus teacher's speech turns in four activities

entire class throughout the session. Also the theme of Activity 4 may have lacked sufficient dramatic tension. As a result, it did not evoke as many effective utterances from the students as the other three activities. (See Chapter Two for the discussion of dramatic tension.)

Teacher's and Students' Initiative Levels

In order to understand how the participants involved themselves in the conversations, we analyzed their verbal data according to the four categories of discourse initiation we have classified: (A) topic management, (B) self-selection, (C), allocating the next speaker, and (D), sequencing the activity. Figure 3.3 displays a graphic comparison based on the results of our analysis. An interesting interaction pattern emerges from this comparison. A significant 44 percent of the new topics (Category A) was initiated by the students. This indicates that the teacher was not the only person who had the power to decide what discourse topics should be included or excluded in the conversation. The students also actively participated in making these decisions. Consequently, although the teacher is responsible for choosing the themes and framing the activities, the drama was built up by contributions from the whole class.

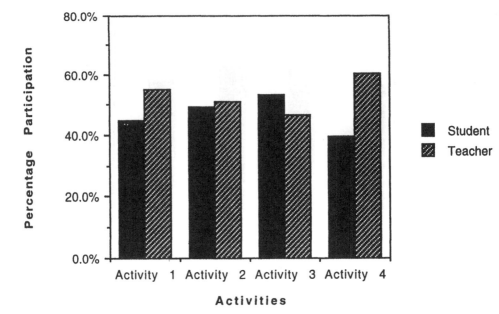

FIGURE 3.3.   **Percentage of students' versus teacher's participation value in the four activities**

The second observation of this interaction pattern is that the students were interested in taking the floor as the drama unfolded (Category B). About half of the time, "selection to speak" originated from the student group in our study. The students volunteered to speak if they needed to express themselves. The students' motivation to speak was derived from the nature of process drama, in which they had strong reasons to communicate with others in order to make the situation move forward to achieve their individual goals. This finding provides evidence that drama activities create an environment in which the interaction pattern between the students and the teacher can go beyond the familiar IRF discourse pattern in an L2 classroom.

The third observation is that the students seemed very active in sequencing discourse and activity in the conversation (Category D). To engage in effective sequencing, according to van Lier, one has to contribute a turn that is either the opening or the closing part of a sequence of discourse or activity. We can see that in drama the students take the opportunity to initiate or close moves in addition to supporting the teacher's opening moves in the conversation (see Figure 3.4).

The students' performance in allocating the next speaker (Category C) was far less effective than the way they performed in the other three initia-

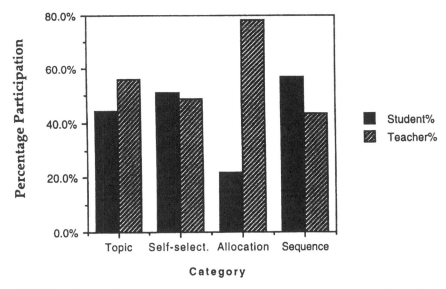

FIGURE 3.4.   Students' versus teacher's percentages of categorical participation in four activities

tion areas. In fact, the teacher was still dominant in this particular type of discourse initiation during the drama activities. This interesting phenomenon can be explained in the following ways:

1. the students were incompetent in allocating the next speakers, regardless of the language used;
2. the interaction format of these activities restricted the students' active participation in this particular initiation area; or
3. the conventional sociolinguistic rules governing ordinary teacher-students interaction influenced these students' attitude in the conversation whenever the teacher was present.

Effects of Different Drama Themes on Participation

In order to understand how different drama themes affect the participants' performances in the classroom, we compared the teacher's and students' participation levels in each activity (see Figures 3.5 through 3.8). As we examine further the differences between these interaction patterns, patterns, it is obvious that the students participated much more actively in

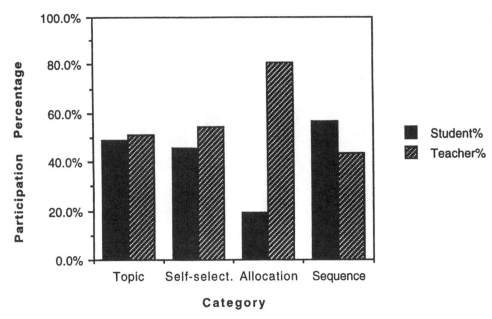

FIGURE 3.5.   Students' versus teacher's percentages of categorical participation in Activity 1—B.B. Wolf

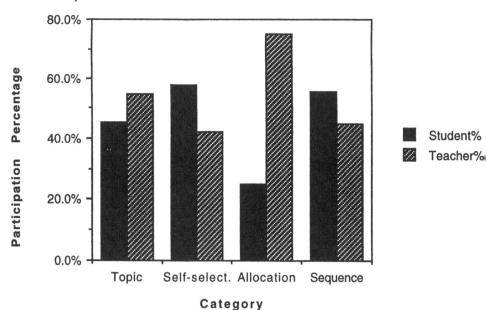

FIGURE 3.6.   Students' versus teacher's percentages of categorical participation in Activity 2—Martial Law

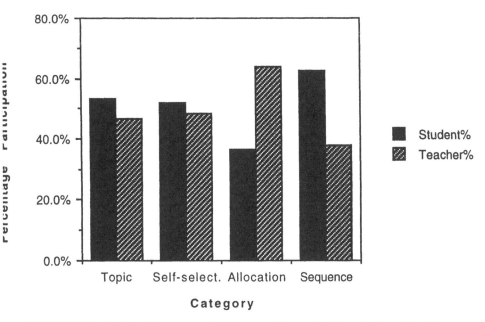

FIGURE 3.7. Students' versus teacher's percentages of categorical participation in Activity 3—Rhino Horns

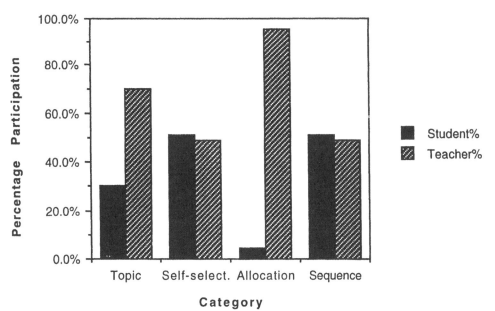

FIGURE 3.8. Students' versus teacher's percentages of categorical participation in Activity 4—Salesmen

Activity 1—B.B. Wolf, Activity 2—Martial Law and Activity 3—Rhino Horns than in Activity 4—Salesman.

In Activity 4—Salesman, the student group initiated very few topics (30%, compared to the teacher's 70%) and did very little allocation work (less than 5%, compared to the teacher's more than 95%). The effort the students devoted to obtaining the floor and managing the discourse and/or the activity was also less significant compared to the way they had performed in the other three activities. Our first assumption was that the significant differences between the two parties' performances in Activity 4—Salesman, compared to the other three activities resulted from the different drama themes: imaginative or realistic. However, this did not seem to be a satisfactory explanation, because both Activities 3—Rhino Horns, and Activity 4—Salesman, had realistic themes, yet produced very different interaction patterns. Therefore drama themes are not the most critical variable in the differences in the participants' verbal behavior in drama.

To obtain a more complete picture of how the teacher and students interacted in the different drama activities, a comparison of the discourse quality and quantity contributed by these two groups was made. Table 3.3 evaluates the performances of the teacher versus students in speech turn percentage (i.e., discourse quantity) and participation value (i.e., discourse quality) during the two types of drama themes: imaginary and realistic.

In terms of discourse quantity, the students took more turns than the teacher during the four activities. Two different distribution patterns of turn-taking were found. One corresponds to Activity 2—Martial Law, and Activity 3—Rhino Horns, and the other to Activity 1—B.B. Wolf and Activity 4—Salesman. The higher percentage of speech turns contributed by the student group in Activity 2—Martial Law, and Activity 3—Rhino Horns, indicates that these two activities created more opportunities for them to

TABLE 3.3.

Summary of Students' versus Teacher's Participation in Quantity and Quality in Different Drama Themes

Drama Themes	Students vs. Teacher Participation	Imaginative Themes		Realistic Themes	
		Activity 1 B.B. Wolf	Activity 2 Martial Law	Activity 3 Rhino Horns	Activity 4 Salesman
Discourse Quantity	Students TT%	56.90%	61.80%	62.90%	57.50%
	Teacher TT%	43.10%	38.20%	37.10%	42.50%
Discourse Quality	Students PV%	44.97%	49.10%	53.20%	39.59%
	Teacher PV%	55.03%	50.90%	46.79%	60.41%

speak in the conversation than the other two activities. In terms of discourse quality, it is not easy to identify any clear patterns from the four activities. The students produced the most effective speech in Activity 3—Rhino Horns (obtaining 53.20% of the total participation value) and the least effective one in Activity 4—Salesman (obtaining 39.59% of the total participation value). Interestingly enough, both Activity 3 and Activity 4 have realistic themes but these two activities seemed to create very different environments for teacher-student interaction. These results indicate that a simple classification of the drama themes (i.e., imaginative or realistic) is not sufficient to explain the participation differences.

A more careful examination of the complex characteristics of each activity is needed. According to our observation, internal tension appears to be one of the most influential factors in the student-teacher interaction patterns. The tension is partially generated from the activity format. Activity 1—B.B. Wolf, Activity 2—Martial Law and Activity 3—Rhino Horns shared a similar format which required the students to make decisions on urgent issues through debate. This decision making created a certain degree of internal tension regardless of the different drama themes. Activity 4, which was different in format from the first three activities, required the students to discuss and report what they had done in the pair work. This less dynamic format possesses little internal tension, and therefore did not elicit active participation from the student group.

The internal tension also arises from the conflicts among the roles. For example, in Activity 2—Martial Law, the learners, who were in role as the residents living in Pond City, were facing the dilemma of having or not having martial law. On the one hand, martial law may provide them some protection in the night; on the other hand, it enforces many restrictions in their life. The conflict increased when the majority of people were against the martial law, but a small group of people who enforced the law (i.e., the general and her two assistants in this drama) were actually in charge of this issue. As the participants debated the issue, internal tension arose which consequently encouraged the participants to take part in the conversation actively in order to fight for their rights. Compared with Activity 3, Activity 4—Salesman did not contain any urgent issues that might seriously affect the participants during the two group sessions: the residents of a community complaining about the annoying salesmen in the community meeting and the salesmen discussing how to improve their selling skills in the company. Since the internal tension of these two sessions was low, the participants did not feel the need to involve themselves actively in the conversation and the participation level dropped.

There was a short pair activity before the two group sessions we used for the participation analysis in Activity 4. In the pair activity, one student, in role as a salesperson, tried to persuade the other student, in role as a resident in a community, to buy the goods. According to our observations, this pair work was much more successful than the two group sessions, in the sense that the salesmen worked very hard to promote their goods and the potential customers were reserved about buying things. The conflict increased and so did the internal tension. The students also reflected in their learning logs that they enjoyed this pair activity very much because of the challenges—to sell their products or to reject the other party. Unfortunately, we were not able to record the conversation of each pair due to some technical difficulty. However, how students interact with each other in pairs or small group activities is an issue worth further investigation.

In addition, individual student's preferences for different topics and his/her understanding level of these topics also affect the participation level. For example, if a learner likes one particular issue or possesses related background knowledge about this topic, he/she will be more interested in participating in the drama than in activities with unfamiliar topics. We will give a more detailed discussion of this issue in Chapter Four.

The Growth of the Students' Communicative Competence

In order to evaluate the growth of students' communicative ability, we designed a special oral test for this study. The test itself was a story-telling task, in which the test taker was required to give a complete and detailed account of what happened in a set of pictures to a listener who needed to arrange the order of the pictures according to the speaker's description. The original idea for this story-telling test came from two sociolinguists, Gorge Brown and Gillian Yule (1983). They pointed out that a task-based oral test like the one we used in this study would allow the teacher to set up a basic scoring procedure for determining how much required information is communicated effectively. We tape-recorded the speaker's speech for the evaluation. The outcome performed by the listener—the order of the pictures one arranged—was not evaluated in this particular test, because we were only interested in the speaker's performance in communicating ideas. Thus, the role of the listener is to create an authentic communicative environment in which the speaker's purpose was to get the information through.

In order to evaluate the growth of students' communication ability during this course, we gave all participants one test before they started the course and another one after the course was finished. Four and seven pictures were selected, respectively, for the pre- and post-tests (see Figures 3.9 and 3.10). The students' verbal protocols were scored in two phases: the clarity of their speech and the number of communication units (CU) each account contained.

FIGURE 3.9.   Pictures of pre-course communication ability test

FIGURE 3.10. Pictures for post-course communication ability test

Analysis of speech clarity

The clarity of a participant's speech was measured according to how detailed the description was. The points reflected how explicit the account of the story was in terms of the location, character(s), action, mental status, and other aspects of the character(s) in the picture. We used the scoring procedure of the post-course evaluation as a further illustration of how data were quantified. Each candidate was asked to describe the events in a set of pictures (see Figure 3.10) to a naive listener. Dialogues (3.11) and (3.12) show how two subjects, S#32 and S#3, described the first picture in the sequence.

S#32: First, there is a man, he is sitting on the sofa and he is smoking.

(3.11)

S#3: Once a person is in his room, he feel very very cold and then he want to go out and buys some food. (3.12)

Table 3.4 illustrates a scoring matrix of the story created for the post-oral test and the points awarded to the two speakers, S#32 and S#3. The matrix incorporates the details of the first picture, namely, (1) location, (2) character, (3) action, (4) status, and (5) other aspects. Points awarded to the speakers reflect the level of explicitness of the candidate's account of the story. Points were given to students when their verbal accounts were meaningful and understandable to the rater, despite possible mistakes in grammar, sentence structure or divergence from standard pronunciation. The sum of the points students receive for the entire set of pictures is their test score in speech clarity. For example, both S#32 and S#3 received 3 points for Picture 1. They both described the location and character(s) in Picture 1, but S#32 was able to tell his listener what happened (i.e., "sitting on the sofa" and "smoking") while S#3 gave comments on the mental sta-

TABLE 3.4.
Scoring Matrix for Picture 1 of the Post-Course Oral Test

Details	Scores of S#32	Examples	Scores of S#3	Examples
Location	1	on the sofa	1	in his room
Character	1	he	1	a person
Action	1	sitting; smoking	0	—
Status	0	—	1	feel cold; want to go out
Others	0	—	0	—
Total of Picture 1	3	—	3	—

tus or feelings of the character in this picture (i.e., "he feels very very cold").

The reason for choosing the modified testing technique for this particular project was that the participants' oral communication ability when they entered the research site was low. The course was designed to help them develop the ability to express their ideas and thoughts through drama activities. The speech data elicited in this type of oral test provided the researcher with exact information about the learners' L2 development in describing events. We did not evaluate the listener's performance because it was not only determined by the speaker's description, but also influenced by the listener's listening ability. The total scores of the pre-course and post-course tests, 29 and 37, respectively, were transformed to percentage scores for the convenience of later statistical analysis.

Analysis of communication units

The evaluation of the student's verbal protocols was based on the numbers of communication units produced in each account. One communication unit (CU) is defined as the smallest meaningful segment in a verbal account. Because the pre- and post-tests contained different numbers of pictures to be described (i.e., 4 and 7), the raw CU scores of the students were transformed to percentage scores for the analysis.

Reliability of the scores

Two independent raters were invited to score the data obtained from the two tests. The percentage of agreement between the two raters was 90 percent. We then took the average scores of the two raters for our later discussion and statistical analysis.

Results

Two *t*-test procedures with matched pairs were run to examine whether there were significant differences in quality—the clarity of the student's speech account, as well as in quantity—the number of CU produced, of the students' oral production between the pre- and post-test (see Table 3.5). The results of the analysis on the subjects' speech clarity show that $t = 5.38$ is significant at .0001 level with $df = 32$. The findings indicate that the students made a significant improvement in expressing themselves. The results of the analysis of the communication units contained in the subjects' speech indicate that $t = 4.19$ is significant at .0002 level with $df = 32$. The findings show that there is also a significant improvement in the students' speech quantity (see Table 3.5).

The results reveal that the students were able to express themselves more clearly and also produced more communication units in their oral

TABLE 3.5.
Summary of the *t*-Tests of the Percentage Scores of Clarity and Communication
Unit between the Pre- and Post-Tests

Variable	N	Mean	SD	Minimum	Maximum	t	P
Difference in Speech Clarity	33	7.97	8.49	−7.12	24.37	5.38	.0001
Difference in CU	33	0.99	1.35	−1.17	3.96	4.19	.0002

performance on the post-test compared with their performance on the pre-test.

Process Drama as a Powerful Version of Communicative Language Teaching

Research findings from this study indicate that this group of learners showed a great interest in participating in conversation by taking more than half of the speech turns. The students also contributed a large number of new topics, volunteered to speak, and were actively involved in discourse/activity management. Clearly, conversation in drama is not completely controlled by the teacher—an advantage in comparison to the teacher-student interaction in more traditional pedagogical tasks. Since drama unfolds with the cooperation of the teacher and students, no single participant is dominant in the activity; as a result, drama is less likely to produce "restricted language" (Colyle & Bisgyer, 1984) in the classroom. Moreover, instead of using fixed discourse roles, as found in other classrooms where the I-R-F structure is detected, the teacher and students have more flexible relationships and negotiable roles in drama conversation. The discourse environment is much closer to real-life situations where all speakers are assumed to have equal rights of participation.

The oral proficiency of the students in this study was considered low when they entered the research site, although they had studied English for quite some time. It is interesting to examine the relationships among their previous experience in learning English, their performance in drama activities and the learning outcomes. Since their knowledge of English was mainly obtained from mechanical practices, drills, and deductive analysis of grammar in high school, their knowledge was static and could not be put into practice in an appropriate environment. Drama, therefore, functioned as an activator in this particular classroom. The students could experience the use of the target language functionally in different contexts created in drama. The students' static knowledge about the target language was activated by the interactive atmosphere and they applied what they had previously learned so that they could communicate their meaning and make meaning from the conversation.

SUMMARY

This chapter argues that conducting classroom-based research into the effect of drama approaches on language teaching and learning is necessary for L2 teachers and researchers to know more about what is happening in such a classroom. Empirical evidence shows that the nature of teacher-student interaction in drama activities resembles real-life communication. Drama approaches are effective in breaking through most conventions of classroom talk and are powerful in creating an equal-rights status of communication. Since classroom conversation, for many language learners, is their major source of learning to use the target language, the unique learning environment created in drama is particularly important.

Current studies have focused on describing and analyzing the use of language and the nature of interaction in drama activities. Future research must generate more empirical evidence in terms of the ways in which different types of drama approaches work and to what extent these approaches can be used for different purposes of language teaching and learning. Clearly there are still many other factors affecting the learner's learning processes, besides taking part in drama activities. The next chapter will discuss the psychological impact of drama experience on learning and teaching, and thus enable us to look at the issue from a different angle.

4

The Learners in the Interactive Process: Psycho-Social Impact of Drama on Learning

And so a language class is one arena in which a number of private universes interact one another. Each person is at the centre of his or her own universe of perceptions and values, and each is affected by what the others do.

(Stevick, 1980, pp. 7–8)

INTRODUCTION

In Chapter Three, we discussed the asymmetric discourse relation between the teacher and learners found in many traditional L2 classrooms, which greatly deviates from the way people normally communicate in real situations. The results of our discourse analysis confirm that a more equal and natural teacher-student interaction is promoted in process drama activities. This educational environment can effectively shorten the distance between the real world and the classroom, as well as to activate learners' "static" knowledge of the target language by pushing them to apply what they have previously learned for meaningful communication.

Indeed, our analysis in the previous chapter merely focused on describing the measurable outcomes of classroom interaction—those which can be directly observed and documented for analysis, such as participants' utterances and physical movements in drama activities. According to our

previous discussion, the ways in which drama-oriented classrooms are organized and materials presented are identified as two major factors in altering teacher-student discourse relationships. However, as both researchers
and educators, we are also aware that the learners' mental state can be
greatly influenced by exposure to process drama in the classroom. This
chapter will shift the focus from analyzing participants' discourse to their
psychological transformation during the interactive process.

The starting point of our investigation is to regard any L2 classroom as a
community and the teacher and students as the members of this community. Based on this perception, we will explore the social and psychological
impact of drama activities on the class as a whole and on participants as
individuals. Then we will discuss how this impact has influenced the members' perceptions about themselves as learners or teachers in this community. The data for our discussion include the participants' oral and written
reports,[2] questionnaires, interviews, and the researchers' observations
from drama lessons we conducted. We also incorporate other relevant
studies as well as our own field experience with different levels and types of
L2 classes.

DRAMA APPROACHES AND HUMANISM IN SECOND LANGUAGE EDUCATION

Popular Beliefs About Using Drama in L2 Classrooms and Some Questions Arising From Them

We have asked many language teachers, who use drama either regularly or
occasionally, why they favor such an approach in teaching foreign languages. One point most of them mentioned is that drama activities bring a
"different learning atmosphere" to their classrooms. Two related questions
were: what specific elements does drama contribute to this difference, and
why is this difference important to second language learning? Generally
speaking, most of our interviewees agreed that the dynamic nature of
drama activities creates a lively, enjoyable learning environment, motivates
students to participate in classroom activities, and helps to build up the students' confidence in learning the target language. Responses like these
are, of course, not merely these teachers' assumptions but arise from their
actual experience of using drama and their observation of students' performance in their own classrooms.

However, their statements about their learning experiences seem not to
be sufficient to convince those who are waiting for empirical evidence

because many essential questions regarding the impact of drama on language learning remain unanswered. Since learning a second language with a group of co-learners in a formal setting is a mental and social process, we are interested in investigating the following:

1. How does drama influence particular psychological and social aspects of participants' learning process?
2. How do drama approaches affect the classroom as a community?
3. What kind of classroom atmosphere is created when drama is used and why?
4. What is the relationship between this particular classroom atmosphere, students' learning process and their classroom performance?

Without systematic research into these questions, the argument about the power of drama will not lead to a productive debate between those who favor it but cannot defend their views sufficiently and those who regard it as "kid's stuff." It is therefore not surprising, that, although the use of drama and certain drama techniques have been promoted for some time, "finding acceptance of these ideas has not been all that easy" (Via, 1987, p. 206).

Components of Humanistic Language Teaching

Although popular beliefs about the power of drama lack empirical support in a rigorous sense, drama teachers' observations have provided researchers with a direction from which to start the investigation. Their experience clearly demonstrates that the greatest power of drama comes from its influence on the participants from within. That is, process-oriented drama approaches promote intrinsic learning. This characteristic is the essence of humanistic language teaching.

Humanistic language teaching reflects an educational philosophy which promotes growth in self-awareness, interpersonal sharing, and intellectual development. Its concepts and philosophy of learning arose from the active debate on educational institutions in the late 1960s and early 1970s. Carl Rogers, one of the most important contributors to the debate, argued that the excitement of learning and teaching is lost in many educational institutions owing to their emphasis on cognition—or "education from the neck and above"—and neglect of the people, their feelings and their transformations involved in the educational process (Rogers, 1975, pp. 40–41). Therefore, the foundation of a humanistic classroom cannot be built merely on estimating what learners can do and evaluating what learners finally produce but on helping them discover themselves as important members of the educational community, valuing their emotional growth, and thus developing their full potential in learning. (See the articles of Stevick, Brumfit and others in Brumfit, 1982.)

Innovative educational approaches and projects of humanistic language teaching have boomed since the 1970s: the Community Language Learning approach developed by Curran and colleagues based on their psycho-therapeutical experience—views the language class as a community in which learners build up trust and interactive relationships with other members to enhance language learning (e.g., Curran, 1976; Stevick, 1980; Rardin et al., 1988), the Silent Way developed by Gattegno—emphasizes that learning is facilitated if the learner discovers rather than remembers what is to be learned (e.g., Gattegno, 1972, 1976), Suggestopedia proposed by Lozanov—creates relaxing environments to enhance language learning (e.g., Lozanov, 1979), Communicative Language Teaching which has been the "buzz" term in our profession over the past two decades (see part one and elsewhere in our previous discussion), Whole Language Approach derived from first language education—stresses that true learning proceeds from whole to parts, (e.g., Altwerger et al., 1987; Freeman & Freeman, 1992) and the process-oriented drama approaches we propose here. Apart from the fundamental educational philosophy of humanism they share, all these teaching approaches or concepts encourage students to offer their own material as the basis for learning, promote self-awareness and reflection, and create opportunities for interpersonal sharing (also see Chapter Five for further comparison of these humanistic approaches). These components function to minimize the four types of alienation from learning suggested by Stevick (1976): The alienation of the learners from the material, from themselves, from the class, and from the teacher, which may be responsible for some of the failures in modern language teaching.

One salient component in drama, which clearly distinguishes it from all the other humanistic teaching concepts, is the characteristics of *make-believe* in drama. In drama activities, participants are deliberately removed from the realistic *here* and *now* situation. That is, our normal perception of the classroom as a physical space for conveying subject-matter information has been challenged; the fixed social status of the teacher and students are purposely altered. Instead, imaginary contexts are created in which the participants act or speak according to the roles they are in. Experiences of different spatial situations and interpersonal relationships are provided for the participants through these imaginary contexts. Reflection and self-awareness are promoted through these experiences as the drama unfolds. Therefore, while some humanistic approaches, such as Community Language Learning and the Silent Way, try to create an open, intimate and non-threatening learning environment by encouraging learners to reveal their *true selves* in interaction, drama approaches achieve the same goal by involving participants in various *imaginary roles* that may violate but also shelter the true selves of the learners in different make-believe settings. This special component becomes a key factor in the change of classroom climate, interpersonal relationships, and individual transformations in a drama-oriented language classroom.

When Reality Meets Imagination

The concepts of reality and make-believe appear completely opposite to each other; however drama activities join these opposites together in the classroom. In daily life we play and encounter different roles in various social contexts. We change our status—teacher, student, parent, child, friend, stranger, employer, employee, and so on—according to whom we are with, what the topics are, and where the events occur. We also adjust our attitudes, tones, speech styles, and word choices according to the social conventions and people around us. We play familiar roles with little extra attention to speech and behavior; as to unfamiliar roles, we may have to practice them over time and obtain experience through trial and error.

In the normal classroom setting, we play our roles as teachers or students based on certain social expectations. For example, the teacher is given the right to summon any student in the classroom and will expect a proper response from this particular student, but none of the students has equal power over the teacher or other students. Furthermore, our society has different expectations about teachers and students—including their manner, ways of speaking, behavior, and even their dress style in school. This *here and now frame* prevents language learners from encountering the target language in different social contexts other than the familiar school setting.

Drama activities, however, successfully break the fixed social rules of the formal school setting by inviting the participants to experiment with different roles under various imaginary conditions in a very safe manner. Trying things out in drama is pleasant and non-threatening for L2 learners because they face the tension of making decisions without the pressure and fear of "how if I am wrong?!"

To elaborate this point, we take the following drama as an example. Once we worked with a group of third graders as their guest teachers in a French immersion school in a midwestern American city. The theme we picked for the students was an imaginary school trip to France. The scene started with the substitute teacher (the researcher in role) taking this group of students to visit the French countryside on a bus. Experiences like this are very familiar to students of this age group. The children got excited when the teacher invited them to "get on board" and naturally sat in rows in the empty space of the room as if they were on a bus. When the teacher suggested they should do something during the long ride, the children immediately decided to sing their favorite French songs together—just like they would on a real school trip. The teacher then pretended to look out through the window of the bus and asked the children about the objects they could see on the journey. The children excitedly mentioned items they had previously learned such as "cows," "farmers," "houses," and so on. However, some playful students saw animals like "tigers" and "elephants" which could not possibly appear in the French countryside. The teacher immediately pretended to be angry and said that good students would never make fun of the teacher. The teacher's purpose was clear: although they were in role in a created context, the scene should not be disrupted by too much inappropriate language.

Suddenly, a student claimed she saw snowflakes. This brought a sudden change in the drama. The bus stopped. The teacher went out to check the bus with the driver and came back a while later to announce that their bus was stuck in the snow. The driver seemed to have run away after he found out it had broken down. The teacher looked very upset and told the children she did not know what to do. One student shouted that he saw a dim light in the dark and perhaps the light came from the farmhouse they had just seen on the way. The teacher then suggested that they should send somebody to the farmhouse to ask for help. The students started a heated discussion about who should go on the mission. The teacher said she would like to go but she had to stay on the bus with the rest of the students. She asked if there was anyone brave enough to undertake this mission. Finally two students volunteered to go together. The scene then shifted to the farmhouse where the two children met a strange old lady—their regular French teacher in role. The two children tried to describe their problem and found the old lady had no telephone and lived in the isolated farmhouse by herself. At last, the lady agreed to lend them her only horse so they could ride the horse to the nearest village to ask for help from the villagers.

This group of students had experienced many incredible challenges in this drama, for example, the bus was stuck in snow, the driver ran away, who should go to look for help . . . , and so on. The two students who volunteered for the mission also faced many unexpected problems, for example, the old lady was not friendly, she was not able to help . . . , and so on. However, these students tried to solve all these problems with their imagination: seeing a dim light in the dark, suggesting somebody should ask for help from the local farmers, negotiating with the old lady to borrow her horse, pretending they could ride the horse . . . , and so on. When the students came to the end of the drama, they had gained a feeling of accomplishment because they had done something brave and, more importantly, they used French to solve problems! In drama, reality and imagination merge. This particular feature allows the L2 learners to use their social skills and imagination to solve problems or make decisions without the constraints of reality.

A SURVEY OF THE PSYCHOLOGICAL IMPACT OF DRAMA

Susan Stern (1981) conducted an informal survey of how different drama approaches affect language learners from a psycho linguistic perspective. Her study was based on the assumption that participating in drama activities helps L2 learners improve their communicative competence. Stern's assumption arose from her review of literature in the fields of drama education for native speakers, psychodrama, and dramatics in speech therapy. She found that despite different aims, each of these areas employs drama because it facilitates communication. Stern elicited several possible psychological factors mentioned in the literature she had reviewed and hypothesized that these factors have a positive influence on L2 learners' development of communicative competence. The factors she proposed include: *heightened self-esteem, motivation,* and *spontaneity;* moreover, *increased capacity for empathy;* and *lowered sensitivity to rejection.*

In order to discover whether these factors have influenced the development of learner's communicative competence, a questionnaire was administered to 24 non-native speakers of English enrolled in three ESL university classes where two types of drama activities were used: short scenes from plays and improvisations. An open-ended questionnaire was also given to the teachers of the three classes to collect their opinions on their objectives and the effects of using drama in their classrooms. Tables 4.1 and 4.2 summarize the students' responses in Stern's study regarding the usefulness of drama and their reactions to drama.

The results indicate that students felt that participating in drama activities, particularly in improvisations, made them feel less embarrassed than other types of classroom activities when speaking in front of a group. Consequently, they believed that they gained self-confidence in speaking. These students also felt very positive about their ability to express themselves and their English intonation when speaking in drama activities. They had enjoyed participating in drama and were motivated to participate further. These students had little difficulty in understanding the characters involved, and they had few problems in identifying with the roles of the characters in the drama.

The teachers shared a common view about the positive effects of drama on these students' learning. These teachers all pointed out in their written responses that not only their active students but also those who were pas-

TABLE 4.1.*
Usefulness of Drama as Perceived by Students

Item on Questionnaire Part I#	Potential Area of Usefulness	Class A X (n = 13)	Class B X (n = 6)	Class C X (n = 5)	Overall X (n = 24)
	Improving Pronunciation				
1-a	Scenes from plays	3.5**	3.2	3.6	3.4
2-a	Improvisation	2.7	3.2	3.4	2.95
	Improving Intonation and Expression				
1-b	Scenes from plays	4.6	3.2	4.2	4.1
2-b	Improvisation	3.6	4.0	3.6	3.7
	Gaining Self-confidence				
1-c	Scenes from plays	3.9	4.2	4.0	4.0
2-c	Improvisation	4.3	4.2	4.2	4.25
	Becoming Less Inhibited or Less Embarrassed When Speaking in front of a Group				
1-d	Scenes from plays	4.3	4.0	3.6	4.1
2-d	Improvisation	4.4	4.7	4.2	4.33
	Increasing/Enriching Vocabulary				
1-e	Scenes from plays	3.0	3.4	3.4	3.0
	Learning More about American Culture				
1-f	Scenes from plays	3.0	3.0	4.2	3.2

Notes:
* The data in Table 4.1 correspond to the items of Part I of the Questionnaire
** The figures are based on the following Likert Scale responses:
   1 = not useful; 2 = a little useful; 3 = somewhat useful; 4 = Quite useful; 5 = very useful
Source: Reproduced from Stern, 1983, p. 90

sive and shy, initiated as well as responded to dialogues "when they stepped out of the classroom into an imaginary setting and situation" (p. 95). These teachers also felt that their students' speech became fluent and their intonation and inflection more native-like, especially during improvisations. These teachers' perceptions about their students' learning outcome are consistent with the students' own perceptions about themselves as learners and speakers in drama activities.

The most interesting finding in her study is that both the students and the teachers believed that language learning benefits more from improvisations than from scripted role-plays. This is quite different from the general belief that practicing lines over time helps learners to lower their anxiety level, increase their confidence, and consequently arrive at more satisfactory results in the final stage. The subjects of this study emphasized

TABLE 4.2.*
Student Reaction to Drama

Item on Question- naire Part II#	Topic	Class A X (n = 13)	Class B X (n = 6)	Class C X (n = 5)	Overall X (n = 24)
Sec. 1					
1	Ability to express self in English during performance	3.2**	3.2	4.0	3.3
Sec. 2					
2	Difficulty in understanding characters	1.5***	1.7	1.1	1.7
3	Nervousness when participating in dramatic activities	2.5	3.2	2.0	2.6
4	Difficulty in identifying with or stepping into role of character	2.4	2.8	1.8	2.4
5	Embarrassment when acting	2.45	3.3	2.2	2.6
6-a	Enjoyment when acting scenes from plays	4.1	3.8	4.0	4.0
6-b	Enjoyment when acting improvisation	4.2	4.2	4.0	4.1
Sec. 3					
7	Evaluation of own performance	3.6****	3.2	4.0	3.8

Notes:
* The data in Table 4.2 correspond to the items on Part II of the Questionnaire
** The figures in the first section are based on the following Likert Scale:

1	2	3	4	5
Overall I was displeased with my ability. I felt very frustrated.				Overall I was pleased with my ability. I felt I was able to express myself with ease.

***The figures in the second section are based on the following Likert Scale:

1	2	3	4	5
not at all	a little	some-what	quite	very much

****The figures in the third section are based on the following Likert Scale:

1	2	3	4	5
I don't like it. It was worse that I thought it would be.		about average		I liked it very much. It was better than I thought it would be.

their positive feelings toward those drama activities which contain more variables and surprises. It is really the different types of tension existing in improvisations, such as the pressure of reacting to others' speeches promptly and solving unexpected problems, that become positive motivation for the students.

CHARACTERISTICS OF THE TRANSFORMATION
OF INDIVIDUALS AND THE CLASS

Based on our discussion of the rationale for using drama approaches, we will focus our discussion on the following features that drama brings to the classroom and investigate how these influence individual participants and the class as a community:

1. Changes in classroom climate;
2. Building confidence in speaking;
3. Opportunities for self-expressions;
4. Individual differences in performance;
5. Making connections with real life;
6. Students' potential in speaking and their communicative strategies;
7. Teacher-students and student-student relationships in discourse; and
8. Some negative attitudes toward drama.

THE CHANGE OF CLASSROOM CLIMATE

Let us first visit one drama-oriented language classroom. The physical setting of the room is what may impress the visitor most at first glance: chairs and desks are not set in orderly lines and rows facing in one direction, but placed in a circle or a half-circle with an empty space in the center. Therefore, students are not sitting stiffly facing their teacher and other students' backs; they are in a circle so that they can see each others' faces easily. The teacher is not standing on the platform in front of the class so to give commands but sitting with the students in the circle like all the other members of this community. In fact, this is only one possible way to set up a drama classroom. Sometimes, a small group of four or five students gather to perform an activity they are given; sometimes, all students are doing actions together in the middle of the empty space.

The only rule of setting up a drama classroom is: there is no fixed rule! The space is arranged according to the needs and contexts of different activities. This flexibility of spatial management completely violates our normal perceptions about what a classroom must look like. The physical change of the room is only the first and the easiest step in conducting a drama-oriented class. However, the dramatic change of classroom atmosphere at this point is instant and quite noticeable. The participants' distanced feelings towards each other and the activities to be introduced are gradually replaced by a more informal and intimate interpersonal relationship in the classroom.

Compared with this first step, eliminating the students' alienation from a new approach that greatly differs from their previous learning experience, is a much more challenging task for the teacher. It is also the most critical step when this approach is introduced to the class for the first time. Unlike the physical rearrangement of the room, the students' mental transformation from resistance to acceptance has no clear-cut timeline and is very learner-dependent. If the students have previously experienced any form of communicative language learning approach, taking part in various drama activities is not a very big shock to them. Otherwise, it may take a very long period of inner struggle for the students to overcome the gap between their previous and present learning styles. The students' open attitude towards drama approaches is the key to further developing a harmonious learning climate.

BUILDING CONFIDENCE IN LEARNING

Among the four alienations Stevick discussed, the students' alienation from themselves as language learners may be the toughest obstacle for them to overcome during their learning process. When learners, adolescents or adults, start learning a foreign language in a formal setting, they are first attracted by the unfamiliar sounds and structure of the new language and then are enthusiastic in imitating what they have heard or seen. At this stage, the learners' strong curiosity about the new language and initial motivation in learning usually enable them to make their first attempt at trying out what they have learned. However, their attempts are not always perfect. Sometimes, these unsuccessful efforts are explicitly corrected by the teacher or their peer learners. Sometimes they recognize their own imperfections when comparing their utterances with those of native speakers, their teachers, or more advanced learners. Feelings of frustration and insecurity arise. When the learners have unrealistic expectations about their achievements in learning, their disappointment toward themselves as language learners accumulates even faster. In this case, the learners' confidence is greatly damaged and their self-esteem becomes extremely low. It is not surprising to hear complaints like: "I am the poorest learner in my class!" or "I can never catch up with my classmates" from our students. Process drama, however, is very powerful in reducing this type of alienation by helping the learners to build-up or restore their confidence in themselves. We shall illustrate this point with the following two case studies.

Case One: Mrs. Chen's Drama Experience

Mrs. Chen was a beginning-level ESL learner originally from China registering in a church-organized weekend conversational program in a midwestern American city. We were invited to work with Mrs. Chen's class for two weeks as their guest teachers and were attracted by her performance in drama. Mrs. Chen was placed in this beginning-level class with five other students—two other Chinese, one Japanese, one Russian and one Korean adult learners—to learn conversational English with the help of two American teachers. The goal of this program was to help adult ESL learners to survive in an English-speaking society and gradually to understand American culture. Their regular class activities were mostly discussions on realistic and cultural topics such as shopping in the supermarket or American traditional holidays.

The drama theme we prepared for this group was "animals and their relationships with human beings." The six students and their two regular teachers were grouped in four pairs, one in role of a pet and the other, as the owner of the pet. After five minutes of pair discussion on the physical features and habits of the pets, the owners were invited to bring their pets to a TV talk show, in which they would introduce their pets to the audience and share their experience of pet-raising. The imaginary pets brought to the show by our guests included a cute rabbit, a beautiful panda, a hungry crocodile and a white sheep. While the owners were talking about their pets, the animals also took an active part in the conversation. They expressed their opinion about the treatment they received from their owners (of course, the animals could speak human language since this was a magic show!). We noticed that Mrs. Chen was the least fluent speaker among the six learners. Looking very nervous and shy, Mrs. Chen stopped frequently to consult with her neighboring Chinese classmate in their own language while introducing her white sheep to the audience. However, all the participants paid attention to her introduction and many laughed when she said she kept her sheep in the back yard because the sheep could eat the grass, so her yard was always very tidy. She seemed to be greatly encouraged by the response of the class and became much more relaxed. Mrs. Chen responded to her classmates' questions such as "what else do you feed to it?" and "what does it look like?" in short and fragmented sentences, but without further help from her Chinese neighbor.

After the class, one of the regular teachers told us that this was the first time Mrs. Chen had spoken so much and so clearly in the class since she had attended the program. The teacher was very surprised at Mrs. Chen's performance in this mini TV talk show. She told us Mrs. Chen usually remained silent during class discussions. Occasionally, she would respond to the teacher's questions in Chinese with a few English words, and her Chinese friends would then translate her sentences into English for the teacher. The teacher had tried many ways to encourage her, but Mrs. Chen always apologized for her poor English with a shy smile. This teacher had been wondering how much Mrs. Chen understood of what was going on in the class.

We were interested in what made the change in Mrs. Chen's behavior in this mini drama, and decided to interview her. This rather informal interview was conducted in her native language during the coffee break. Mrs. Chen said she did not feel particularly nervous as she usually would in the class, because telling people about the imaginary pets was very interesting. She said she was usually embarrassed to speak English in front of her younger classmates because "they all know (she) made many mistakes." We then asked her how she felt in this mini drama. "It's different!" she said. She told us the only thing in her mind at that moment was to search for the right words to describe her "sheep." "It's quite funny," she said, "the more I talked about it, the more I felt my partner sitting beside me was just like a real sheep!" According to our observation, Mrs. Chen seemed to follow the proceedings of the scene very well. She laughed or nodded when other people were describing their pets, which would be unusual for a less competent learner like her in traditional teacher-oriented activities. The participants' rich facial expressions and the body language accompanying their descriptions may have greatly contributed to her understanding. More importantly, Mrs. Chen herself was one of the "playwrights" of the drama. It was her scene!

Mrs. Chen's drama experience reminds us of two interesting features of process drama:

1. The created contexts ease the beginning learners' anxiety because the pressure of "speaking well" or "doing it right" does not exist; and
2. Involvement in the imaginary roles helps low-proficiency learners to forget about their fear of speaking in public, because the message they convey is more important than the linguistic forms of the message they use.

The effectiveness of process drama in terms of raising the learner's confidence level also depends on the size of the group and the format of the activity. When the class size is much larger than the case we have described above, the anxiety level of less-confident learners increases. It is, consequently, more difficult for these learners to break the ice in front of a big group. Beginning-level learners may feel much more comfortable speaking in pair- or small-group activities because their utterances will not attract as much attention as in the big group. We have noticed that our less confident students usually speak and perform much more actively in pair- or small-group activities than in the class-based ones. Speaking is, of course, not the only form of participation. Less fluent learners attempt to support these activities with their physical movements, such as using hand gestures and body language, before they overcome the fear of speaking aloud in the class.

Case Two: Jen's Drama Experience

The drama experience of Jen, a university student, reveals a slightly different story from that of Mrs. Chen. Jen was one of the 33 Taiwanese first-year university students participating in our semester-long case study discussed in Chapter Three. She graduated from a very prestigious girls' high school which was nationally known for its students' outstanding academic achievement. According to our pre-course survey on the students' previous learning experience, Jen obtained 50 (the full score is 100) on the English subject test of the Joint College Entrance Examination (JCEE), which was slightly lower than the mean of the class (Mean = 54.41), and much higher than that of all exam takers of that year (Mean = 37). However, Jen had very little confidence as an English learner. She gave herself '1s' for her speaking, listening, and reading skills and a '2' for her writing skill on a 6-point Likert Scale where 1 was "very poor" and 6 was "very good." In fact, Jen's communication ability was not as poor as she believed. Her performance on the pre-course communicative competence evaluation showed that she was above the class average. The test required her to describe a series of pictures to a listener, so that the listener could arrange the order of the pictures accordingly. Her clarity score—evaluated according to the details of her description—was 55.17, and the score of communication units—the number of smallest meaningful units in her description for each picture—was 3.5, both exceeded the mean scores of the class (47.02 and 3.05, respectively) on the pre-course evaluation. (See Chapter Three for the details of these tests.) In other words, Jen's actual language proficiency level was higher than her self-evaluation reflected.

The teacher found that Jen had very impressive communication skills. Although she did not have a rich vocabulary, she was able to use alternative ways to express herself. Jen's first reaction to the teacher's positive comments on her performance was: "How can that be? My English was always at the bottom of my class!" It seemed Jen's self-esteem was extremely low due to the highly competitive learning environment in her high school. Jen also admitted that she had no interest in learning English because memorizing grammar rules or doing drill exercises endlessly bored her very much in the high school English class, and she often failed in the exams. "I had been very scared about this Freshman English course before it started," she wrote in her journal, "because I was afraid I will fail again in the university."

As the course went on, Jen's interest in participating in classroom activities increased. Jen was actually a very active student. She found that speaking with her partner in pair activities was quite interesting, because her partner could understand what she was trying to say. Then she realized that speaking in front of the class was not as difficult as she used to believe. She discovered that the objective of learning English in this course was communication, not merely taking exams. The variety of drama activities and their dynamic nature fascinated her. She was happy that with the help of some gestures and body language her "broken English" was easily understood by her classmates. She started feeling proud of her performance and wrote, "I feel good because I was the first person to say something in today's class."

Jen's performance on the post-test was not as good as we expected. Her clarity score, 54.05, was slightly lower than the class mean (Mean = 55.00) and her score on Communication Unit, 2.71, was also lower than the class mean (Mean = 4.04). It seems Jen made only moderate progress after the course compared with her performance in the pre-test. However, if we look at the two sets of post-test scores from the view of her effectiveness in describing events, Jen's performance in the post-test was not too bad. Her post-test scores shows that within a small number of utterances (Communicative Unit), Jen could convey the information effectively (Speech Clarity). Jen had, at least, learned how to express herself clearly and economically from her drama experience. She had also been one of the most active participants in the class. In the long run, Jen's change of attitude will enable her to actively apply the knowledge of English that she already possesses in authentic communication and will motivate her to make a further step in language learning.

CREATING OPPORTUNITIES FOR SELF-EXPRESSION

In our previous discussion of the mini drama lesson, "TV Talk Show," we mentioned that the regular teacher of the class was very impressed with the students' performance in general and with one less competent learner's unusually enthusiastic participation in particular. This outcome arose from the careful organization of the lesson. This mini drama consisted of two parts. The first part was a very short pair-discussion between two learners, in which they negotiated the type of pet one learner played, including the physical features and characteristics of the pet, and the relationship between the pet and the owner. In the second part of the drama each owner introduced the pet to the "studio audience"—the other learners and teachers.

The function of the pair-discussion is to encourage the learners to come up with ideas together as the basis of their later speech. For less fluent speakers, listening to their partners' ideas and exchanging information with each other can prepare them for their public speech in the later group activity. They can organize their thoughts as well as their partners' ideas in the pair work time so that they can make a better presentation later. The confidence level of these learners immediately increased when they had something to talk about and, most importantly, when they knew how to express their ideas. Although the skeleton of the talk show was formed by the comments of the "pet owners" about their "pets," all the participants were very attentive to whatever was said since all topics closely concerned themselves. Therefore, it was not surprising that the "pets" also actively participated in the show because they also wanted to express their opinions about the comments their owners made. This type of lesson organization is particularly effective for creating opportunities for self-expression in big classes and consequently it will promote intrinsic participation.

Many learners have told us in their written responses or during interviews that they felt more relaxed and thus more involved during small-group or pair-work time than during big-group activities. This is a very interesting reflection because learners can indeed take more speech turns when they have only one or two interlocutors. Furthermore, the learners also have an obligation to initiate topics or respond to others' topics during pair-work time. Pair-work in process drama is not the same as that in usual classroom activities in its purposes and functions. Pair-work in drama often functions as a "prelude" to another activity. During the pair-work, the two participants define the roles (e.g., the two learners discussed the characteristics of the pet in the "TV Talk Show" activity), or develop sub-storyline within the roles they are given (e.g., one learner, in role as a policeman, interviewed the other learner, in role as a forest animal, about what happened when the big bad wolf visited the three pigs in the "B. B. Wolf" drama). The content of their conversation is crucial to the development of the drama in the following activity (usually group-based). The participants are often very involved in the pair-work which is, therefore, an ideal format to increase opportunities for self-expression and communication. Unfortunately, most available studies have focused on the participants' performance during whole-group activities. It is thus necessary to collect data from drama containing pairs or a smaller number of speakers, to understand how participation patterns differ from those found in whole-group activities.

INDIVIDUAL DIFFERENCES IN PERFORMANCE

Based on our observation, learners' participation levels may not be as consistent as many teachers believe. In others words, some learners may remain active or inactive throughout the course but most students participate in drama with varying interest according to their individual familiarity levels and preferences toward different drama themes, formats, or even the roles involved. To examine this point further, we need to look at how individual learners perform in a drama-oriented course over a longer period.

Figures 4.1 to 4.4 show how 33 university students participated in the four drama activities in our semester-long case study presented in Chapter Three. These students' participation indices were sorted and plotted for each activity. Their overall performances are presented in Figure 4.5 where the sums of their participation indices were stacked and sorted. Some students are consistent in terms of their participation level throughout the course. For example, Student 14 and Student 19, who achieved the first and sixth positions in the overall participation ranking, were also evaluated among the top third most active students in each of the four activities. However, some learners performed rather differently in each activity. Student 10, for instant, had obtained the third highest participation index in the overall analysis but did not give any verbal contribution in Activity 1 (B. B. Wolf) and was not much involved in Activity 3 (Rhino Horns), either. Student 30, who was the second most active learner in the overall ranking, did not give any verbal contribution in Activity 1.

We were curious about possible factors influencing individual students' different performances in our case study and reviewed the class records (including the tapes and the teacher's field notes) and the students' journals. We found that there was a close relationship between the level of students' involvement in the roles they took and their participation levels. For example, Student 10 was extremely active in Activity 2 (Martial Law), in which he volunteered to be the assistant officer to the teacher—in role as the General. He reflected in his diary that he found the role extremely challenging because he did not know his mission would be to defend martial law which he personally did not agree with. He wrote, "However, I must perform the duty since I was a soldier, and I did try very hard to convince those who were against the martial law! My classmates teased me that I was the 'claw' of the dictator after class."

The second factor we found in our case study was the students' attitude to and knowledge of the selected topics. For example, Student 22 who was more active in Activity 1 (B. B. Wolf) than in Activity 3 (Rhino Horns) revealed that the issue of Taiwanese businessmen stock-piling rhino horns discussed in Activity 3 was not very interesting to her because she seldom read current issues in the newspaper. "Although the teacher had assigned a newspaper article to prepare us for the activity," she wrote, "the whole event seemed to be very far from me and thus was difficult for me to say anything during the class." On the contrary, the background story of "The Three Little Pigs and the Big Bad Wolf" in Activity 1 intrigued Student 22 and thus raised her interest in expressing her views. She revealed it was because she was impressed by how this familiar story could be interpreted by the participants in such different ways.

Although a learner may participate in one activity more than another due to the various idiosyncratic factors we have described above, the

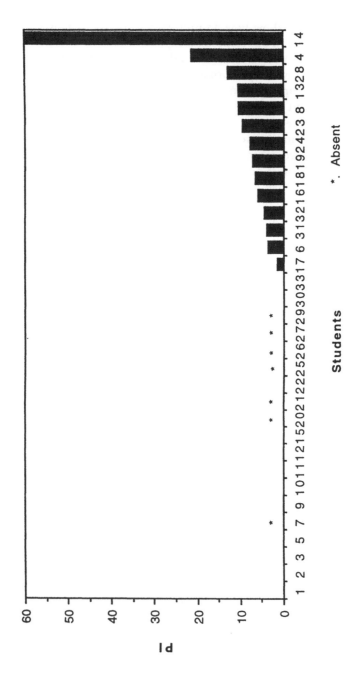

FIGURE 4.1.   Sorted student participation in Activity 1—B.B. Wolf

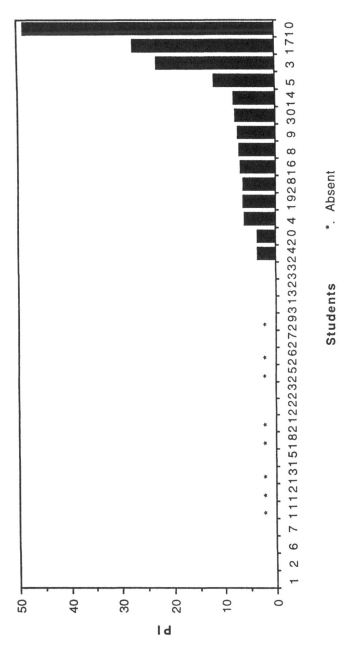

FIGURE 4.2.   Sorted student participation in Activity 2—Martial Law

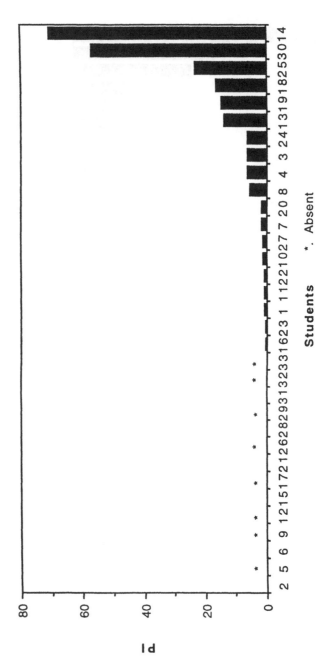

FIGURE 4.3. Sorted student participation in Activity 3—Rhino Horns

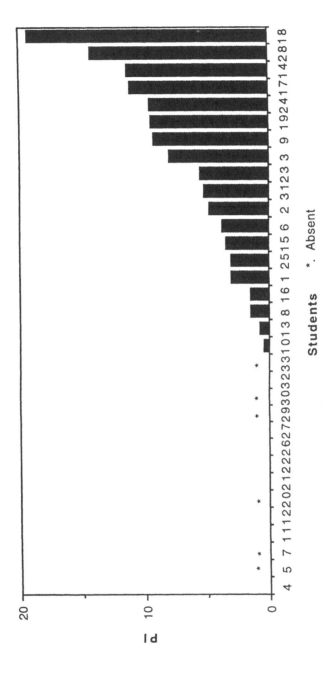

FIGURE 4.4. Sorted student participation in Activity 4—Sales Men

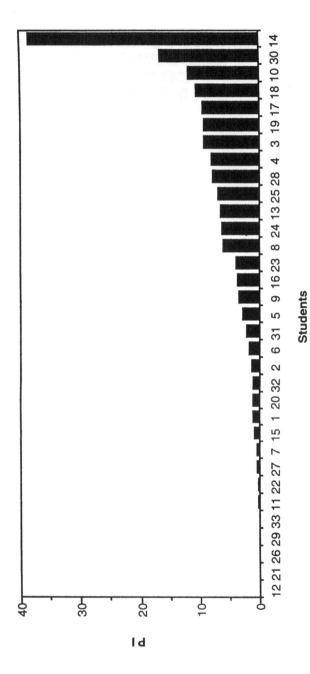

FIGURE 4.5.   Sorted student participation in four activities

learner seems to interact with others in a rather consistent personal style. That is, some learners may be good at initiating topics while others may be competent in seeking opportunities to speak. Therefore, by analyzing how one learner performs in the four initiative areas—topic, self-selection, allocation, and sequencing—across several activities, we can find the learner's particular interaction pattern. Figures 4.6 to 4.9 present stacked graphics for four particular students in the same case study, based on their participation values in each of the four categories across the four activities.

Generally speaking, all four students did best in sequencing work and worst in allocating their next speakers. Each student's personal style is clearly shown in the graphical analysis. Comparing these graphics, we found that Students 3 and 4 seem to share a similar style while Students 8 and 10 represent another type of interaction. Student 8 and 10, for example, were better at getting the floor than at initiating topics while Students 3 and 4 could perform better in starting new topics than in volunteering to talk in a big-group conversation. Of course idiosyncratic differences remain within each particular pattern. Students 10, for example, was extremely competent in seeking opportunities for speaking, which is unusual among all other students in this class. Analyses of this type provide valuable information to the teacher in understanding each students' strengths and weaknesses in interaction so to help them acquire the necessary skills for communication.

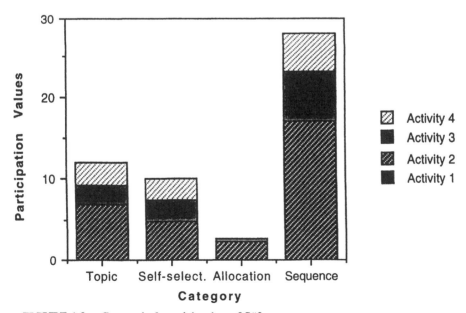

FIGURE 4.6.   Categorical participation of S#3

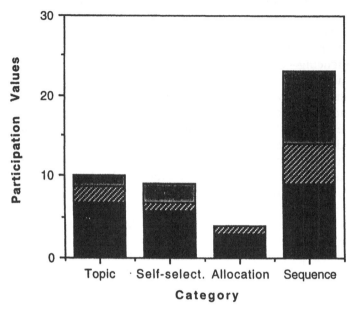

FIGURE 4.7.   Categorical participation of S#4

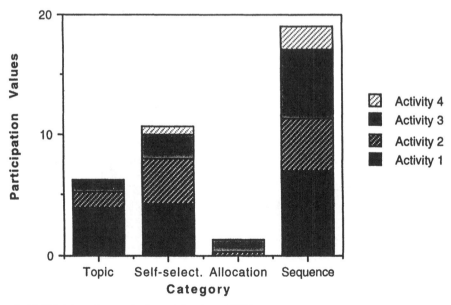

FIGURE 4.8.   Categorical participation of S#8

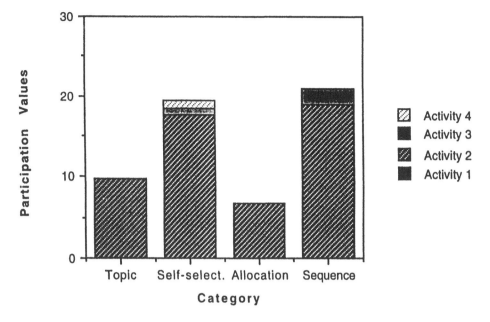

FIGURE 4.9.   **Categorical participation of S#10**

MAKING CONNECTION WITH THE REAL LIFE

Process drama was originally developed to help children in first language settings to understand themselves, people around them and the world they are living in. In other words, by taking on imaginary roles, contexts, and different themes, children are able to connect their drama experiences with what may occur in their real lives. Although this aspect of the power of drama has not received particular attention in second language education, promoting understanding about the world is indeed the key to successful classroom activities in a broader sense. A unit of process-oriented drama lesson is, in fact, a form of content-based curriculum design because the unit is usually centered on a specially selected theme which conveys educational information to a certain group of learners. Therefore, the goal of conducting drama activities in an L2 classroom should not be limited to language development but upgraded to the level of promoting connections with the society and culture of the target language, thus linking the learners' experience in drama directly or indirectly to the real world.

We will elaborate this point from our experience of working with the university-level learners in the study discussed in Chapter Three (see also Kao, 1994). These students expressed their understanding about their drama experience in their learning logs. The theme of the drama unit we picked for this group of learners was developed from a children's picture book—*Tuesday* (Wiesner, 1991), which tells an imaginary story about frogs flying on water lily leaves in the sky of a small town one Tuesday night.

In the first lesson of this unit, a scene was developed in which residents of Pond Village (an imaginary place) found thousands of water lily leaves scattered all over the town one Wednesday morning. A police investigation was carried out and many people claimed they had heard unusual sounds and witnessed strange flying objects on the previous night. The class was divided into two groups—one group played journalists and the other, residents (human as well as animals) of the city. Each journalist interviewed a resident about what happened on that night and made an oral report to the chief editor (the teacher in role). The results of their interviews were very interesting: some people believed there was a scientific experiment going on in the nearby research institute; others argued that a group of UFOs had visited their town; and still some others thought it was a bad joke by some crazy people. There seemed no definite evidence to point toward any of these explanations.

The second activity for this unit was "spreading rumors." Students, in-role as the villagers, walked freely in the empty space of the classroom and whispered gossip about the weird night they had heard from others into other villagers' ears. The rule was: each person starts with his/her version of a rumor and then keeps spreading whatever is told to him/her. At the end of the activity, the whole class sat down and shared the latest version they had heard. It was very interesting that the original stories had changed a lot during the process of passing them around in the classroom. Many students wrote about how they felt taking part in the process of "spreading rumors" and some made a connection with what they often did unconsciously in real life. One student wrote

> I experienced the power of rumors in today's activity. To tell you the truth, it was fun to make up a story at the beginning because I wasn't very serious about it. But I was very astonished how my story had changed after being retold several times! This reminds me of a painful but true experience of mine. I happened to be one of the people involved in spreading gossip among my friends. Me and one of my good friends had a misunderstanding about each other due to these gossips and were both hurt deeply. I now understand how rumors are formed. Sometimes, things are out of your control.

To this group of students, participating in this activity helped them to understand how some social interactions may have a great influence on people's lives.

The drama continued to the third activity, in which the teacher, in role as a military general, announced the enforcement of martial law in a citizens' meeting where all the students participated as local residents. The students who agreed or disagreed with the conditions of martial law presented their arguments and debated the positive and negative influences of the law on their daily lives. Students who disliked martial law were particularly active in confronting the General and her assistants (two voluntary students) about its unreasonably strict conditions. Finally the General agreed to have a citizen vote on the issue but tried to manipulate the results. This ending provoked indepth reflections on what democracy and justice meant to the students in their written journals. This unit of drama was far more influential on the students' understanding of democracy and people's relationships than discussing any text on these topics.

STUDENTS' POTENTIAL IN SPEAKING AND THEIR COMMUNICATION STRATEGIES

We communicate in order to get the message across. In other words, communication is a continuous process of expression, interpretation, and negotiation through speed and gesture. Language is only a part of the communication process because our interlocutors understand the message from our facial expressions, eye signals, hand gestures, and physical positions along with the words we say, the voice we produce, and the tone we select. This is how messages are conveyed in everyday situations and in drama activities in L2 classrooms. Some learners express themselves with linguistically inappropriate forms due to their limited proficiency in the target language; some others may chose socially unacceptable terms in the target culture. Both the teacher and learners are, however, often surprised by how much potential the learners demonstrate when they are actively involved in drama situations.

Relying heavily on body language, spelling out words, writing down phrases, or even drawing pictures are some of the common strategies found among less competent learners. Some L2 learners will also provide many expressions or examples associated with their intended meanings when they do not possess appropriate vocabulary. In order to make sure their messages are understood, many L2 learners like to repeat their utterances, especially when they lack confidence in the way they phrase themselves.

The following dialogue demonstrates how a group of beginning-level ESL adult learners interact with each other using various communication strategies. In this segment, S1 (a female Chinese learner) was introducing her "big rabbit," S2 (a male Chinese learner), to the imaginary audience of a TV show hosted by the researcher (T). S3 a male Japanese learner was also a pet owner and Ab (their American teacher) was S3's pet. The topic under discussion was the diet of S1's rabbit:

Dialogue 4.1[3]

S1	57	let me see...because in China, a lot of rabbit just eat grass, so I don't..American rabbit eat what..., maybe cho::..cho:..cho:..
Ab	58	chocolate!...hahahaha::..
S2	59	nonono! ((shaking his right hand))
S1	60	I don't know American rabbit eat wha:t..
T	61	why don't you ask your rabbit
S1	62	yeah.yeah..maybe, I think, this rabbit, rabbit very like rice!
SS	63	((laughter))
S2	64	rice only? I am a BIG rabbit..((bending his arms to show his muscles like a superman)) I need power! I want to eat MEA::T!
SS	65	((laughter))
T	66	we have a rice rabbit here..
S1	67	I think, I think this rabbit very much like the rice..and any and any, any [flui:t]?...[flui:t], right? [flui:t]...like apple, or orange..or [flui:t]...
S3	68	but rabbit do not drink what kind of.
S1	69	but right! rabbit is very like..he is very like [flui:t]..like apple..((using her left hand to form the shape of an apple))
S3	70	oh, yes, yes, but do not drink wa:ter..((shaking his head))
T	71	((turn her head to S1)) don't give him any...drink because, he said rabbits don't drink water
Ab	72	don't drink water, yes..((nodding her head))
S2	73	ye:a, yeah.((nodding his head)).
S3	74	yes, especially rabbit do not drink water or ju:.., jui:ce::..((holding his right hand as if he has a cup in it))
T	75	((to S3)) what would happen if you give..
S3	76	rabbit is drink the vegetable water...

Our attention was first attracted by their rather exaggerated body language, for example, shaking and nodding heads to indicate disagreements and agreements or using hand gestures to help describe objects and concepts. Moreover, their dramatic changes in tone and rich facial expressions not only added flavor to the roles they were in, but also hinted at the meaning of their speech for their listeners. Using body language to help communication is, in fact, a naturally developed skill for L1 speakers during the process of learning how to interact with people in their native culture. This group of learners obviously applied this strategy to the L2 setting in a much more noticeable manner. They think dramatic body movements and changes of intonation can compensate for insufficient language ability in communication. Our observation shows that L2 learners' enthusiasm for using body language diminishes when they speak in more traditional classroom activities, such as answering teacher-controlled questions or performing drill-like exercises. This is because the essential reason for using body language—the need to get the message across—does not exist in these traditional exchanges.

The second issue that interests us is what strategies L2 learners may adopt when they encounter different types of linguistic difficulties in communication. Let's take S1 (the owner of the rabbit) in this dialogue as an example. S1 obviously had difficulty with the pronunciation of the word "fruit" throughout the talk. Her hesitation was first noticed in Turn 67. She first repeated the word several times but realized that other participants were still puzzled about what she was trying to say, so she changed her strategy by giving examples to clarify the confusion: "[fru:it]. . . , like apple, or orange. . . . " Unfortunately, S3 (another pet owner) misunderstood [flui:t] as "fluid" and thus advised S1 not to feed her rabbit with liquid: "rabbit do not drink water" (Turns 68 and 70). There is no way to know if S1 had realized the misunderstanding between her and S3; however, S1 kept emphasizing the food she fed her rabbit was something "like apple." Her strategy of repeating and emphasizing the sound "[flu:it]" indicates her lack of confidence about the pronunciation or even spelling of the word she intended to use.

It is also interesting to see how learners' native languages play a role at both semantic and syntactic levels while communication proceeds in the target language. For example, S1, a native Chinese speaker, consistently applied the syntactic structure of her native language when constructing English sentences. The structure of her statement-like question: "I don't know American rabbit eat what," meaning "I don't know what American rabbits eat," in Turns 57 and 60, and that of her statement: "I think this rabbit very much like rice," meaning "I think this rabbit likes rice very much," in Turns 62 and 67 closely resembles Chinese word order. There are two possible explanations of why this strategy has developed:

1. S1 did not have the knowledge of certain types of sentence structures in the target language, such as the structure of the English indirect question in Turn 57; or
2. Although she had learned these sentence structures, she did not know how to apply her knowledge in real situations; thus she naturally resumed her native language system.

These two situations also occur at the semantic level. L2 learners may "borrow" phrases from their native language or even "create" new terms based on their interpretation of the concepts they want to express. For example, S3, a native speaker of Japanese, created a new term, "vegetable water" in Turn 76 to express the concept of "juice contained in a vegetable." Amazingly, other participants did not seem to have too much difficulty in understanding S1's Chinese English or S3's "creative" new term, though they had different cultural backgrounds (there were also two Americans, a Russian, and a Korean among them).

We interviewed S1 after the activity, trying to understand what her problems were when communicating with people in everyday situations and in the classroom. S1's response was rather interesting. She told us that her husband, a graduate student studying in a nearby university, encouraged her to improve her English by preparing for the TOEFL test. "It was not too difficult to remember words or to read texts," she said, "but I didn't feel my spoken English was improving. I have problems putting words that I have memorized into sentences when I speak with others." She told us she could usually take her time to think how to phrase her sentences when answering her teacher's questions in the class, but did not have this luxury in real situations because her interlocutors seldom had patience like her language teacher! "You couldn't review your grammar in front of a supermarket cashier when there is a long queue behind you, could you? And then my sentences become broken." she said. We asked her what might improve her spoken English; her answer was "Speak more often!"

ESL adult learners who do not work or study in the target language environment have very limited opportunity for regular contact with native speakers. They might have enough vocabulary and might even have the knowledge of how sentences *should be* constructed but lack appropriate *contexts* to apply what they have learned. Unfortunately, if they use inappropriate structures or invented phrases, these may become fossilized in their interlanguage system during the learning process. This problem is particularly serious for learners in foreign or immersion settings where all learners share the same native language. "Classroom pidgin" is thus developed in the long run if no appropriate help is provided for these learners.

Strategies developed by L2 learners in drama activities resemble those used by them in real communication. These strategies help them maintain the flow of discourse exchange with other speakers, increase their fluency in speaking and also indicate where their problems are at the linguistic level. Language teachers should address the learners' problematic usage or sentence structures within meaningful contexts during the reflection session, so that the learners will be aware of appropriate forms when they encounter similar real-life situations.

TEACHER-STUDENT AND STUDENT-STUDENT DISCOURSE RELATIONSHIP IN DRAMA

Our everyday interaction is regulated by the social rules pertaining to the particular context in which the conversation takes place. The ways in which speakers take turns, select tones, decide about speaking styles, and make word choices are determined by their interpersonal relationships with the other participants, as well as by the discourse topic, time and place involved. L2 learners who are already competent in their native language often bring their knowledge in conversational rules—acquired in their native cultures—to the contexts where they use the target language for communication. For example, L2 learners from most Asian cultures where there are strict rules for speaking to people with a superior social status because of their professional level, family, or moral status, often apply this understanding in the L2 classroom. It is natural for these student to use "respected forms and manner" when speaking to their teachers who are supposedly superior to them in all aspects.

Transferring the strictly-set teacher-student interactional conventions from the L1 culture to the already teacher-dominated language classroom (see our discussion in Chapter Three) not only prevents learners from actively participating in the classroom conversation, but also creates an obstacle for learners in experiencing how to talk with people in different situations. The unequal interactional relationships between the two parties will remain the same as long as the participants are "wearing their social masks" set up by the society. However, in drama all participants are given opportunities to drop their set masks; indeed, everyone has the chance to try on different masks and speak according to a different social status.

Let's take as an example from our analysis on how the teacher and students interacted in drama in our case study (see Chapter Three). The results of our analysis of teacher-student performance in the four discourse initiative areas show that the students were fairly active in initiating conversational topics, volunteering to speak, and organizing discourse or activity sequence (see Figures 3.4 to 3.6). The level of the student's involvement in these three areas was comparable with that of the teacher, which indicates that drama had promoted a more equal socio-linguistic student-teacher relationship in conversation. However, it is noticeable that this group of Chinese students was not competent in allocating their next speakers (see Figure 3.7). In other words, the teacher was still dominant in different drama activities in this aspect even when the conversational contexts were deliberately removed from realistic ones. It is intriguing to investigate why drama is not as effective in breaking the teacher's privilege in appointing who should speak next, as it was in the areas of topic management, self-selection, and discourse sequencing.

The four activities discussed in this case study were all whole-group activities that involved the entire class during the interaction (i.e., there were 33 students in this class). Participating in big-group conversations needs sufficient experience and language ability while providing appropriate signals in one's speech to a certain speaker (or a group of speakers) so that this person (or this group) can take over the floor smoothly. To exchange turns successfully with other participants in a big group requires very sophisticated communication skills. According to their reports of their previous experience in learning English, the learners in this study had almost never participated in large-group L2 conversations (and possibly seldom did so in L1 settings) before they entered the research site; therefore, they lacked the experience and appropriate communication skills to allocate next speakers during conversation. According to our observations, these L2 learners performed much better in this aspect in small-group talk (i.e., conversations involving 3 or 4 participants). It would be interesting to compare in a more systematic manner how individual learners participate in small- and big-group talk. Some students also pointed out in their learning logs that they felt particularly tense when the teacher was physically present in the interaction and thus were unable to talk "naturally" as they usually did with their partners in pair- or small-group conversations. Obviously, the traditional image of the teacher as an authority figure was deeply rooted in these learners' perception. These students naturally viewed the teacher as somebody who had the power to dominate the classroom conversation. Therefore, they often hesitated to talk to other students directly during the activities without getting the teacher's "permission" first.

Interestingly, we also found that the more the students became involved in their roles, the less they were influenced by the traditional social rules which govern how the teacher and students would normally interact. In "Martial Law"—one of the more successful activities in this case study—two students who took on the roles of the mayor of the city and a night club owner respectively, started a heated debate on whether martial law was or was not necessary for the city. Many students stood up, forgetting the existence of the teacher, to join in the debate.

Furthermore, the way the teacher presents the role he/she is playing in front of the class also has a great influence on the relationships with the student group. The way the researcher set up her role in the drama: "A School Trip to France" provides a good demonstration here. In order to create a new relationship between the "teacher" and "students" in drama, the researcher—in the role of their substitute teacher—first asked the children: "What kind of teacher do you want me to be?" They replied, "A very nice one!" The researcher immediately took the role of a "nice, sympathetic" teacher who often asked what the students wanted to do on the bus instead of giving them commands or correcting them all the time. By asking this question, the researcher "shared" the authority of "being a teacher" with the students who helped shape the character of the "substitute teacher." The formal, unequal relation between the teacher and students had been changed in the scene; the children became very active in the conversation.

Generally speaking, giving less dominant roles to the teacher, such as a poor old lady or a homeless child, instead of those which traditionally carry superior status, such as a king or a judge, develops a more balanced discourse relationship in drama. Of course, different ways of presenting these roles also have tremendously different effects on the outcome. The teacher in the role of an old, helpless judge, for example, can promote more active participation from the students than a sharp, smart one.

STUDENTS' NEGATIVE ATTITUDES TOWARD DRAMA ACTIVITIES

Our experience of working with different groups and levels of learners shows that drama activities receive mostly positive comments from the participants. This does not, however, mean that drama works for everybody! Some language learners did express negative opinions, directly or indirectly, toward drama approaches. We classify their attitudes into three types.

The first type of student either treats a drama-oriented language class as an "easy-pass course," or regards drama activities as "party time." This attitude is particularly salient among students who have little interest in language learning but must enroll in the course due to school policy or the education system. They are not serious about the course and believe that their duty is limited to passing the course. They welcome the course objectives and classroom activity format because they think they do not have to spend any effort on their school work—reading novels, reciting articles, or memorizing vocabulary and grammar rules in order to pass a pen-and-paper examination—as they usually do in traditional language classes. Students of this type often skip classes since they do not think their absence will affect the results of their learning. Their "take-it-easy" attitude offends those who are serious about learning when they are present and their absence may also have a negative influence on the other students' interest in learning. The number of students of this type is, luckily, proportionally small.

The second type of negative attitude derives from some students' skeptical view and distrust of the drama approach. This attitude is more common among adult learners or students who have received language education in a more traditional manner. Students of this type often have strong doubts about what they can gain from drama because they perceive drama activities as "kids' stuff". We once had students coming to us at the beginning of a course to politely "suggest" that we should not spend too much time on "playing games" but write down vocabulary or do grammar exercises on the board so that they could go back and memorize them at home and prepare for our next lesson! Some adolescent learners are reluctant to participate in activities with fantastic themes because they think doing so makes them look "silly" or "childish"; some shy learners feel scared and uncomfortable when they hear the terms "drama" and "role-play" because their perception of drama remains at the level of "stage performance" or Shakespeare plays. Fortunately, many of these students gradually changed their original views as they got more familiar with the classroom setting and recognized the value of drama as they reflected upon their classroom experience.

The third type derives from the pressure one group of learners puts on the other group by demonstrating their progress in learning through their active participation in classroom activities. Students who have low self-esteem in learning or poor language proficiency levels may easily be discouraged by their active and confident peers during their struggle to learn. Learners of this type often hide themselves silently in the corner when others are actively participating. We would like to discuss this attitude in detail from our observation of one particular university learner—Henry. Henry was a Mathematics major in the study presented in the previous chapter. Henry started learning English at the age of 12 in junior high school but confessed that English had been a "nightmare" for him ever since. He obtained 34 on the JCEE English test, which was one of the poorest scores in the class. He gave himself "2s" on his speaking, listening, and writing ability, and "3" on his reading skill on the 6-scale self-evaluation form before the course started.

Henry usually sat at the back and seldom spoke during class. He wrote in his journal

> Frankly speaking, my English was as poor as a third-year junior high school student . . . I lost my enthusiasm in practicing spoken English when once my high school English teacher asked us to discuss something in English with my classmate. I tried to join the discussion with my broken English, but I felt so frustrated because nobody seemed to understand what I was saying!

In fact, part of Henry's learning problem came from his poor English pronunciation and strong local accent. For example, Henry often skipped the last sound(s) of a word if it was a consonant; therefore he would pronounce "cold" as "/ko/," skipping both "l" and "d." His way of pronouncing English words usually confused his classmates during the conversation. He admitted that he seldom read English texts, not to mention "speaking" in English. Consequently, he had not only had difficulties in expressing ideas orally, but also had a hard time in understanding other's speech.

The lively, informal classroom atmosphere slightly eased Henry's fear and tension; at the same time, Henry also felt tremendous pressure when he tried to participate in activities because of his active classmates' performance. He wrote

> It seemed all my classmates use English to talk with each other. But how about me? Why couldn't I open my mouth? I think I was so afraid that my classmates would laugh at my broken English . . . . This fear bothers me so much that whenever I open my mouth, my tongue get twisted and my brain goes blank . . . . Why doesn't the teacher just ask us to write or read something. Reading and writing are much easier for me than talking.

The teacher did create opportunities for Henry to take part in drama activities. Unfortunately, Henry was not willing to step out of the shell of self-pity. He complained

> The teacher had a pair of sharp eyes. No matter where I hide myself, she was always able to find me and give me something to do.

One of Henry's major learning difficulties was derived from his inability to distinguish and pronounce English words at the linguistic level, which, unfortunately, had a negative effect on his perception and attitude toward the activities at a psychological level. Serious frustration occurred while Henry was communicating with other participants in the activities, which discouraged him from trying again and formed his resistance to drama. It is not easy for the teacher to provide individualized help to a student like Henry in such a big class while the activities are proceeding. However, we found that group rather than individual participation was an effective way to reduce learning anxiety in Henry's case, because a shy and less competent student is usually more willing to express himself when he is not alone in the spotlight. For example, we found Henry was more active in "tableau" where he worked with several classmates in a collaborative manner than he usually was as an individual participant in the big group activities.

Compared with Henry's feelings about speaking in the class, his attitudes toward other forms of activity, such as in-class writing were much more positive. Henry expressed his preference toward writing down his ideas, instead of speaking out loud in the class, in his learning logs. For students with less competent speaking ability, various formats of drama activities provide alternatives for self-expression and participation. Their self-confidence and interest in learning can be restored through participating in the activities they are more comfortable with, and thus a more "balanced," healthy attitude toward all aspects of the course may develop in the long run.

SUMMARY

Individual participants have become the most valuable component in a drama-oriented language classroom. They not only bring their knowledge about the world, their learning styles, personalities, and previous experience in language learning to the classroom but also interact with one another on the basis of the knowledge they possess and they have been developing during the course. The dynamic forms, themes, and atmosphere created in process drama function together as powerful activators which encourage the learners to share and reflect upon their experience and thus promote more interpersonal interaction than in more traditional classroom activities. Different learners are affected differently by this interaction: less competent learners may overcome their fear and frustration in language learning and develop a more healthy, active attitude toward language learning; sensitive learners are able to draw connections between their drama experience and the real world, and develop a deeper understanding about people, cultures, and societies outside the classroom. Learners who have limited access to authentic communication with native speakers also benefit from their drama experience in which they can try various roles, learn social rules of conversation, develop communication strategies, and thus gain confidence in using the language. Most importantly, learners are not simply independent beings in a drama classroom; they contribute to each other's learning process and together form a community in the classroom.

5

Planning a Drama-Oriented Second Language Course

INTRODUCTION

There is a marked gap between research findings and the real effect on the teaching of a second language through drama. The primary reason is the lack of research about using drama in L2 learning and teaching. Obviously teachers cannot wait for slow empirical testing and re-testing research processes on the use of drama; therefore, classes are usually planned from individual experience and not research results. Also, teaching experience cannot be easily accumulated, evaluated, and replicated in different contexts with different levels of learners. Since research designed to investigate the effects of drama approaches on L2 teaching and learning is still in progress, the results of existing research from general L2 classroom studies offer valuable sources for justifying and planning drama-oriented courses. Studies of learning routes and second language development can provide solid evidence for the use of process drama in the L2 classroom (e.g., Brumfit, 1980; Ellis, 1988).

Another reason for the research-application gap is that too much attention has been paid to the *technical procedures* of drama at the course planning stage. Language teachers need to approach course planning with a broader and more holistic vision. Although the needs of different classrooms vary, when planning a course one must consider factors that may influence the implementation from above, such as social context and state policy, and from below, such as teacher-student relationship and students' learning attitude. In this chapter, we will first validate L2 development processes in drama with reference to general models derived from L2 classroom research. Next, procedures for planning a drama-oriented L2 course are discussed, based on the six elements of language teaching: *policy, approach, syllabus, materials, the participants,* and *the classroom.*

THREE COGNITIVE ROUTES FOR SECOND LANGUAGE DEVELOPMENT IN THE CLASSROOM

The learner's output—his/her performance in classroom activities—indicates the results of some complex cognitive processes of internalizing knowledge presented directly or indirectly to the learner. In his Variable Competence Model, Ellis (1988) proposes two sets of cognitive processes contributing to a learner's second language development (SLD): primary processes and secondary processes. Primary processes occur when learners augment their L2 knowledge with their world knowledge of conceptual schema, communicative functions, situational features of discourse contexts, and language organization. The learner's L2 ability develops through a series of stages involving formulaic speech, propositionally-reduced speech, syntactic utterances, morphologically marked utterances and complex utterances. This set of processes helps the learners create discourse in unplanned situations. This developmental route is likely to be found in naturalistic L2 learning and leads to knowledge of a non-analytical type.

Secondary processes contribute directly to analytic L2 knowledge. This set of processes helps learners to make use of existing analytical knowledge and also to add to it. Although knowledge developed through secondary processes is not immediately available for use in unplanned discourse, it enables learners to be sensitive to language forms, and eventually it becomes accessible for communication when the learners' knowledge, developed in primary processes, reaches the utilizing stage. Without appropriate activating processes, their analytical knowledge may remain static and inaccessible throughout their lives. However, this developmental route occurs mostly in classrooms where formal instruction focuses on analyzing language forms and practicing drills.

The route involving primary processes seems to be a possible path leading to effective and authentic communication. However, for most adult learners, who have already acquired their mother tongues and possess sufficient world knowledge, this is not an efficient learning approach in terms of the investment of time and energy. There might be examples of successful "street learning," but the developmental procedure is rather slow and may require enormous efforts in the early stages. Furthermore, this route is likely to lead to pidginized speech that may not cause critical difficulties in everyday communication but is a fatal obstacle for further improvement and refinement of the target language.

Brumfit (1980) proposed an integrated route involving both primary and secondary processes for classroom learning. A lesson unit designed to promote learning through this route should contain both formal presentations of new language items and practice in communicative activities. Both analytical and non-analytical knowledge are likely to develop when these two types of classroom activities are meaningfully combined and support each other functionally. The interaction of the two sets of knowledge will thus speed up the developmental rate of the students and lead to more satisfactory learning outcomes.

SECOND LANGUAGE DEVELOPMENT IN A DRAMA-ORIENTED L2 CLASSROOM

The classroom studies presented in Chapters Three and Four indicate that L2 learners' attitudes, their interaction styles, and the discourse they produce in drama activities resemble real-life communication. In other words, drama provides learners with a very effective environment to develop their L2 through the route involving primary processes. However, it is important to note that most of the participants in our studies—unlike learners in naturalistic situations—already possessed analytical knowledge from their previous experience. Drama activities, therefore, provide them with various communicative situations so that their analytical knowledge evolved rapidly into non-analytical knowledge. In this circumstance, the participants' L1 knowledge and their general knowledge about the world contribute to the success of the communication. The formal instruction they had received in their previous language classes also play a critical role in the learning process. It is clear that when they take part in drama activities, learners develop their L2 ability through an integrated route involving both primary and secondary processes.

However, it may not always be the case that all learners in a group will have acquired appropriate analytical knowledge before they take part in a series of drama episodes. From the viewpoint of effective teaching, it is important to prepare learners for unplanned discourse in a direct and explicit manner before they get involved in their roles in drama. For example, the teacher can discuss necessary vocabulary and certain language structures that are needed for a particular episode with the class. This preparation process need not be formal. It can be embedded within the context of the drama as the preparation was done in the "Street Children" drama (see Chapter One). In this drama, we provided pictures, newspaper articles, and other documents related to the situation of street children in South America as the "pre-text" of the drama. Through reading and discussion, the students obtained necessary background knowledge and vocabulary about the drama.

Because drama activities may develop in unexpected directions, new language elements are likely to occur at any time during the process and may result in difficulties while the learners are attempting to communicate. One solution could be that the teacher temporarily suspends the drama to provide immediate help to the students. In fact, our everyday conversations in L1 are not always smooth and fluent either. Therefore, it is not necessary to stop the activity every time the students stumble or hesitate, unless the obstacles are fatal to the continuation to the drama. Besides, the students benefit from monitoring each other's verbal contribution to the dialogue. Participation itself is a valuable channel for learning the social conventions of the target language. Of course, the teacher must closely monitor the ongoing activity and be aware of the students' communication difficulties.

There should be a short period of reflective time after each drama activity. During this period, new language items that occurred in the drama may be discussed with the class, based on the teacher's observation and the students' reflection upon their drama experience. The group discussion or follow-up assignments can also cover sociolinguistic aspects such as appropriateness of discourse manner, intonation, cultural expressions, and turn-taking. For example, writing a letter to a character created in role in the drama can be a very useful follow-up assignment for the students. This reflective and evaluative phase is critical to the learners' second language development in the sense that it allows them to analyze what they have done in the un-planned discourse. Reflection is thus a compensation for the fact that drama activities initially focus on language fluency and may result in pidginized speech.

Figure 5.1 shows how a learner's L2 knowledge develops in a drama-oriented language classroom based on the notion of the three instructional phases: preparation phase, participating in drama, and reflective phase.

Each phase has its own function but it is closely related to the other two. The preparation phase provides learners with a background for the drama as well as essential language items to be used while participating in the activities. Analytic knowledge is obtained before it is put into practice and will be gradually transformed into accessible knowledge for later real-life communication. Meanwhile, new non-analytical knowledge is generated through primary processes, due to the unpredictable and simultaneous situations and ideas that evolve in drama. The reflective phase allows learners to clarify their new non-analytic knowledge so that unnecessary struggles in language learning are avoided and the learning rate increases. L2 knowledge is built upon the interaction between the processes of forming analyt-

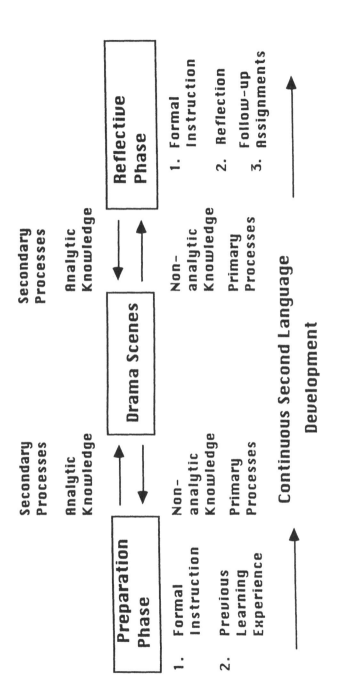

FIGURE 5.1. SLD processes in a drama-oriented L2 classroom

119

ical and non-analytical knowledge when the three phases support one another in function, theme, and purpose.

COMPONENTS OF LANGUAGE TEACHING IN DRAMA-ORIENTED L2 CLASSROOMS

Ellis proposes a general model demonstrating the relations among the components that directly or indirectly shape classroom interaction (Ellis, 1988; see Figure 5.2). At the top of the model is educational policy regarding the objectives of the school curriculum. Below this level is the approach that has been chosen to fulfill the objectives specified, which then determines the syllabus of a particular course, including its organization, contents, and implementation, as well as the evaluation procedures of the course. Appropriate materials are then selected based on the syllabus and brought to the classroom where they are encountered by the teacher and learners. The focal point of Ellis' model is "the classroom because this is where contact between the teacher, the learner, and the materials occurs" (p. 192). Since both the teacher and the learners bring their attitudes, opinions, knowledge, and personality to the teaching and learning process, a certain level of unpredictability always exists in the classroom. Consequently, any course plan must allow for a certain degree of negotiation.

This model offers a starting point when planning a drama-oriented L2 course. The following sections will discuss how this model can be combined with the theory of using drama in L2 teaching and learning, so that a useful guideline can be developed for the teachers who plan to use drama in their classrooms.

Policy

Educational policy is usually a decision enforced from above based on political, socio-economical, cultural, and historical factors. It often determines the nature of other components in this model. For example, in many countries national policy determines what particular languages will be taught and to what extent. National policy may strongly influence the way a course is designed and taught because the outcomes of teaching must fulfill the requirements set by the policy. If the policy advocates communication competence, the teacher is encouraged to help students develop their ability to participate in un-planned discourse in the classroom. Teachers who favor drama in language teaching will feel confident in planning their courses under this type of policy since the strength of drama activities is to create contexts for natural communication. If the pre-

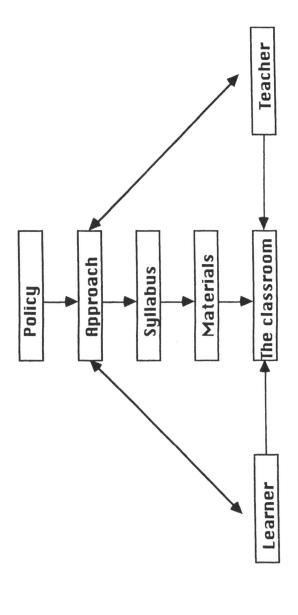

FIGURE 5.2. The components of language teaching
Source. Ellis (1988, p. 193).

ferred approach of classroom practice is in accord with the policy, desired educational goals are easily achieved.

However, in many cases, educational policy requires students to take part in national examinations that emphasize the importance of correct language usage. This type of policy is likely to lead to classroom practice that focuses on formal presentation of the language and thus results in learning through secondary processes. Teachers who favor the drama approach have to overcome two major obstacles before they plan their lessons. First, the theoretical ground of "fluency over accuracy" in drama may cause learning frustration when the students realize that in reality the communication competence they develop in the classroom is not directly related to the examination that will determine their future academic careers. Second, the conflict between policy and classroom practice may further lead to the students' reluctance to take part in any drama activities. To eliminate this discrepancy, new language items must be carefully integrated into the drama, and more emphasis should be placed on the preparation phase and reflective phase in each lesson.

Approach

From the beginning of this book, applying the theory of process drama in L2 education has been referred to as an approach. This provides the philosophical foundation for designing and organizing classroom activities at the practical level. Since process drama is an approach rather than a method, it allows some freedom for individual application according to the local needs, social backgrounds, and perspectives of different classrooms. Although the teacher and students developing a series of drama episodes or scenes together is a unique aspect of process drama, it is based on the same educational ground as many other established approaches.

The philosophy of learning a second language through drama is consistent with some current "humanistic" and "whole person" approaches. Stevick (1982) and Brumfit (1982) argue that in order to learn a second language in a holistic manner, learners need a program that pays more attention to the purpose of their learning, maintains a balance of power between the teacher and students, and adopts methods that assume utility of the theory of learning. The learning atmosphere evoked in drama activities also parallels the psychological bases of "Counseling Learning" (Curran, 1976) and "Community Language Learning" approaches (CLL) (Stevick, 1982; Rardin et al., 1988). According to the CLL approach, learning is "intrinsically a process of interpersonal communication" and is actually "made possible by the quality and structure of the personal relationship" (Rardin et al., 1988, p. viii). Therefore, learning is more likely to take place when there is mutual trust between the learners and the people they are working with. Drama activities also reflect basic principles advocated in the "Whole Language" approach, which emphasizes that learning takes place as the group "engages in meaningful social interaction" and language development "proceeds from whole to part" (Freeman & Freeman, 1992, p. 7). Rather than having the students first memorize bits and pieces of information about the language (i.e., the parts of the language), teachers start the lesson through content by concentrating on key concepts (that is, the whole of the language).

Process drama shares most features with the current notion of "communicative language teaching," in that both stress the importance of learning and using the target language in a meaningful context, and emphasize that learning the descriptive aspects of the target language alone is unlikely to lead to satisfactory communication in real life.

However, it would be problematic to enforce complete correspondence between these approaches because certain differences remain. For example, the CLL approach differs from process drama in that the CLL approach encourages the learner to reveal the "true self" when interacting with other learners while process drama creates a "make-believe" context for the work. It is more appropriate to view the various approaches and methods as a continuum, with the features of "communicative," "informal," "humanistic," "psychological," "fluency-oriented," and "experiential" on one end and "non-communicative," "linguistic," "analytical," "accuracy-oriented" and "traditional" on the other. All the established approaches can be located on the continuum according to their essential characteristics. Process drama will be located toward the communicative end. Its location on the continuum is not fixed; it moves toward either end depending on the way it is implemented in the classroom. If the desired goal of teaching is to prepare students for participating in unplanned discourse, drama can provide the core of each lesson; in this case, this approach will move toward the informal end of the communication continuum. When the desired teaching goal is to prepare learners for performing planned discourse (such as taking some examination), drama may occupy a less significant part of the entire course and the location of this approach on the continuum will move toward the other extreme.

Syllabus

Once process drama is chosen as an approach, an appropriate syllabus can be designed according to the nature of the course; e.g., drama-oriented conversational course, writing course, literature course, or "whole language" course covering all four language skills simultaneously. Generally, a syllabus can involve pre-course or concurrent selection of items. Pre-course selection means that teachers design the syllabus before the course starts, while concurrent selection means that teachers make decisions about what and how to teach as the course proceeds. Due to the unpredictable nature of process drama, a practical syllabus often develops from a combination of pre-course and concurrent selection procedures. Figure 5.3 illustrates the selection procedures for planning a drama-oriented course.

From the viewpoint of planning the scaffolding of a course, the teacher first needs to specify the goals in order to decide if the course will be orga-

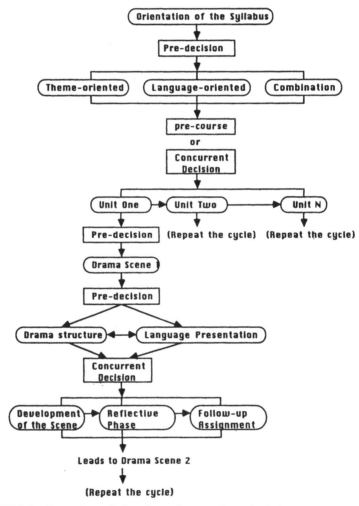

FIGURE 5.3.   Procedure of planning a drama-oriented syllabus

nized on the basis of the themes or the language items to be introduced in drama. The former choice emphasizes the value and meaning of the selected themes for the learners' cognitive development and understanding about the world. Therefore, the themes to be included need to reflect the world of the learners and the implications for the students' lives. Linguistic elements to be presented are selected according to the needs of the drama and the presentation is less formal and often embedded in the activities. This type of syllabus suits the needs of content-oriented courses, for example, reading/writing, literature, or "whole language" courses. The latter type of syllabus, in contrast, centers on the intended linguistic items to be taught during the course. Here, drama activities are designed to reflect the *application* of the particular linguistic elements in meaningful contexts. The themes and meanings in each drama activity or episode are a less critical element in the syllabus. This type of syllabus is better suited to courses that aim to develop the learners' communication competence, such as conversation courses. A combination of these two types provides an alternative orientation for syllabus planning.

After the orientation of the syllabus is decided, the outline of the units or lessons at the working level can be planned accordingly. Some teachers prefer to choose all the topics to be covered before the course starts; others make decisions on a day-by-day basis, depending on a number of different factors: the learners' needs, their interests, their progress, current issues, and so on. No matter which attitude is adopted, the teacher must structure each drama episode before it begins. The *context* of the drama, the *roles* to be created and encountered, and the possible *developments* of each episode should be carefully considered; the quality and quantity of the *linguistic items* to be presented in the preparation phase and the manner of their presentation should also be decided. It is, however, impossible to predetermine every outcome of the drama before it actually begins, because the communication that arises from the drama comes from negotiation and the participation of the whole class. This unpredictable quality is a key element in the learning, and also challenges the teacher when conducting the course. The teacher will have to design the general outline of the drama but will work with the whole class in determining how the drama is to be continued, completed, and followed-up according to what occurs in each scene or episode. The teacher can design the theme and structure of the drama activity but what will actually occur in the drama cannot be predetermined. Any unfamiliar language aspects arising during the activity will then become discussion topics in the reflective phase. The outcome of a scene and the conclusions reached in this stage will then lead to a working basis for the next episode; another cycle of decision making, both preplanned and concurrent, begins.

There is one further point worth making with regard to the planning of a drama-oriented syllabus. A syllabus developed in this way recognizes the value of negotiation among the participants about what to do and how to behave in the classroom. Therefore, all pre-decisions made by the teacher should be open for modification and further development once they are brought into the classroom because new drama ideas or language aspects stimulated in the teacher-student interaction are likely to be the most appropriate source of learning and teaching.

Materials

Selecting suitable materials for a process drama syllabus is by no means an easy task. The most urgent concern is that there are few available handbooks for second language teachers that adequately reflect the process drama approach. One reason is that this approach is so new that writers and publishers have not promptly responded to teachers' needs in this field. A more crucial reason is that any pre-designed "recipe" style textbook may not fit into a drama-oriented classroom where the learning foci continuously evolve from the activities. The primary solution is that teachers select themes from available folk tales, children's books, literature, history, current issues, and so forth, and tailor the raw material for their local audience as the course proceeds. Material developed in this way will best suit the unique characteristics of each classroom. However, this solution is very time-consuming even for experienced teachers.

As a more promising start, language teachers can modify existing materials, lesson plans, or structures, designed for different purposes and levels of native language classrooms. Available publications such as *Drama Guidelines* (O'Neill et al., 1976), *Drama Structures: A Practical Handbook for Teachers* (O'Neill & Lambert, 1982), *Dramathemes: A Practical Guide for Teaching Drama* (Swartz, 1988), *Role Drama* (Tarlington & Verriour, 1991), and *Story Drama: Reading, Writing, and Role-playing across the Curriculum* (Booth, 1994) are designed to develop first language ability, cultural and social understanding, cognition, communication skills, world knowledge and so on from a variety of sources including historical events, literary works, folk tales, and social issues. The themes behind these materials have been carefully evaluated and the procedures have been tested in various L1 settings. The following guidelines are suggested for selecting and modifying appropriate materials from L1 sources for an L2 course:

1. Cognitive appropriateness: Although drama is basically "let's pretend," the themes behind the selected materials must be appropriate to the learners' cognitive level. For example, younger L2 learners may have a more positive attitude toward participating in drama based on folk tales or

children's stories than adult learners who may think these stories "childish" or "cliché." However, with some modifications—for example, creating adult roles and changing the original storyline—the themes in these stories are of lasting interest. Our "B.B. Wolf" and "Martial Law" drama sessions demonstrate how children's stories can be modified for adult learners' interest and cognitive level.

2. Cultural differences: Themes that are familiar to learners from one culture may not be equally effective with another group. Cultural distance from a particular theme is very often the source of student alienation and detachment from participation in the activity. This is not to suggest that a group of learners can only work with themes from their own culture; on the contrary, participating in drama can be a powerful means of understanding different cultures, for example the culture of the target language for L2 learners. The key to the successful transfer of cultural materials is to prepare the learners for the activity before they are in role.

3. Potential for further development: A drama unit usually consists of several scenes or episodes conducted through different drama techniques. Each scene must allow for a certain flexibility because as the situation evolves it is likely to deviate from the original plan. In other words, effective materials will be open-ended in terms of their themes and structures.

4. Evaluation of the quality and quantity of the target language to be used: Available L1 materials are designed according to the basic assumption that the participants, regardless of their ages, are fluent in their native language. Drama activities of this kind require sophisticated language ability, but may not be appropriate to be used in the L2 setting. Beginning level L2 learners, for example, have very limited proficiency, and thus verbal communication is almost impossible in drama. In this case, linguistic items presented to the learners prior to the drama and an emphasis on non-verbal responses in the activities, become very important. Whether the syllabus is oriented towards drama themes or language aspects, the language teachers must evaluate the level of difficulty of the language elements to be used for the intended group before introducing the materials.

The Teacher and the Learners

The selection of material and development process is undoubtedly a critical element in successful classroom practice, but good materials alone will not necessarily guarantee successful language learning. After all, materials are to be used both by the teacher and the learners; only they can determine how effective the materials will be in enhancing learning. Unfortunately, reports about students' resistance to drama approaches are not uncommon, especially at the beginning of a drama-oriented course. This phenomenon has become for many teachers one of the major reasons for giving up drama. According to our observations, there are many sources for learners' resistance, including distrusting a new approach, feeling insecure about the absence of textbooks and the lack of formal instruction, and misconceptions about classroom learning.

We must also recognize that the classroom atmosphere is determined by the teacher's attitude, beliefs, and professional knowledge. In other words, the stance of the teacher will influence the learners in the process of learning. A creative, skillful, and confident teacher is usually capable of motivating learning even under the most disadvantageous circumstance.

If the teacher's stance is to be altered, a few questions need to be answered:

1. What are the necessary qualities of a "good" teacher?
2. Are these qualities inherent or can they be acquired by teachers in training?
3. What can be taught to would-be practitioners of drama in second language education?
4. What areas can be left for the teacher to discover?

Dorothy Heathcote, an authority on drama education, firmly believes "all people can learn to teach well, if they are not put into defensive areas during their training" (in Johnson & O'Neill, 1984, p. 26). She suggests that excellent drama teachers know how to relate to other people and to themselves. These qualities will also apply to those who teach a second language.

To relate effectively to students it is essential to be willing to

1. see the students as they are and recognize their needs;
2. arouse the students' interest and realize their potential;
3. see the world through the students' eyes, but be able to withstand certain pressures from the students;
4. control the situation for the students when necessary;
5. give power to the students and rely on their power; and
6. be slow to make judgments about students and constantly reassess one's opinion of each student.

To relate to self, teachers must be able to give themselves fully to the task in hand; to be themselves and accept the limitations of their situations. At the *professional* level, teachers must possess sufficient knowledge about

1. theater arts and drama techniques;
2. the rules of drama;
3. how to select significant moments in drama;
4. how to handle spoken language and non-verbal signals;

5.   how to create tension; and
6.   the connection between the materials of the syllabus and students'
     wider experience.

In Heathcote's view, good teachers should be sympathetic but powerful, know when and how to control situations in the classroom, keep an open mind, maintain their commitment to teaching, and possess sufficient professional knowledge. We all know that when we instruct the students to "Pay attention!" or "Remember this!" our intended purposes are seldom fully achieved. Similarly, being a friendly, pleasant, and easy-going teacher does not necessarily guarantee successful learning outcomes or the achievement of the desired teaching goals. All these qualities can be taught to teachers in training, but they can be acquired more effectively if teachers constantly review their own experience so to refine their skills and knowledge through actual practice. Teacher's stance determines learners' attitudes toward the course and learning itself. Only when the teacher accepts the new role of a "partner" of the students and firmly establishes the course from this stance, a cooperative relationship among the teacher and students will be built, and thus effective teaching and learning can be achieved.

The Classroom

The classroom is where all the above elements come together. That is also the place where learning happens. A drama classroom should provide a comfortable environment so that the teacher and the students can work together. Tables and chairs may be moved from their traditional positions and easily arranged according to the needs of the created scenes. In process drama, there is no audience, formal costumes, or stage settings; however, small objects such as photos, paintings, or other props may be useful in generating ideas for drama. Symbolic or imagined props are often used. Ideally, drama should take place in a large space. However, many teachers will be forced to work in the limited space of their classrooms, crowded with tables, desks, and chairs. But even these unpromising conditions can be improved by stacking tables, and setting out chairs in a circle. This also gives the signal that the usual classroom atmosphere has been altered.

A secondary issue in the literature of L2 development is the way in which learning is extended from the classroom to the students' lives. Language learning, as we all know, is a continuous and accumulating process. A satisfactory learning outcome is unlikely to be achieved solely within the limited class meeting time. One strength of process drama is that many new directions for further work are initiated, and another strength is that the impact of participating in drama is powerful and motivating for cognitive development outside the classroom. When planning after-class assignments, the teacher should keep in mind that the nature of the assigned work must not be independent of the meanings and contexts of the work that has taken place in class.

A CHECKLIST FOR THE TEACHER WHEN PLANNING AND IMPLEMENTING THE SYLLABUS

Before introducing process drama to the L2 classroom, the teacher should

1. determine the kinds of language tasks the students will be given, such as asking questions, listening to information, sharing information, instructing, describing, persuading, giving orders, speculating, offering explanations, and so forth;
2. prepare students for some of the more unfamiliar language structures or vocabulary items that the context may present;
3. identify the kinds of themes, issues, and topics that will interest and motivate the group, and will be culturally relevant and appropriate;
4. recognize sources of unease in the tasks the students may be set or in the social challenges they may have to face;
5. choose roles for both students and teacher that will maximize language opportunities in the context;
6. select a starting point that will launch the drama effectively;
7. identify the teaching functions that will arise within the drama: organizer, instructor, informant, commentator, questioner, adviser, timekeeper, challenger, and so forth; and
8. maintain sufficient flexibility to go beyond the original planning in pursuit of learning opportunities.

Once the course starts, the teacher should constantly monitor his/her teaching and the students' reaction in the classroom as to adjust the original plan according to actual needs. During the course, the teacher should

1. create and maintain a classroom atmosphere where dialogue is the norm and where students' contributions are accepted and valued;
2. recognize that there are both linguistic and social challenges for the students in a drama activity;
3. accept, support, and if necessary elaborate on students' verbal offerings, rather than immediately correct mistakes;
4. remodel students' language if it is inaccurate or inappropriate;
5. invite students to improve inadequate contributions without rejecting what has been offered;

6. work creatively and appropriately in role, selecting a language mode that will help to demonstrate relevant language styles for the class;
7. offer information, vocabulary, and language structures, if possible implicitly within the drama context, without burdening the students with the teacher's knowledge;
8. diagnose and recall specific weaknesses among students, without emphasizing them during the drama;
9. note areas of difficulty for the students, both social and linguistic, and address these concerns in the reflective phase of the lesson or in a later session;
10. find reading, writing and research tasks arising from the drama that will revisit some of the language items occurring in the lesson, and use these tasks to reflect on the issues that have arisen;
11. recognize that the kinds of learning that arise may not primarily derive from the direct instruction and input of new information by the teacher; and
12. accept the validity of the knowledge, experience and values that students already possess and wherever possible, include these in the work.

SUMMARY

This chapter described the ways in which theory in L2 development—such as Primary or Secondary Processes derived from Ellis' Variable Competence Model—may be helpful for language teachers in planning a course based on process drama. A successful drama-oriented language course should integrate both primary and secondary processes, containing formal presentation of new language items and practice in communicative activities. A general model has been developed for planning a drama-oriented course. In this model the following six components influence each other and shape the outline of the course: policy, approach, syllabus, materials, the participants, and the classroom. Language teachers play the key role in this planning process because their philosophy about the course, attitude toward students, teaching style, methods, professional knowledge, training, and many other qualities all determine the success of the course. Only when the teacher accepts the new role of a "partner" of the students when planning and implementing the course will effective teaching and learning be achieved.

6

Evaluating Second Language Development in a Drama-Oriented Classroom

INTRODUCTION

In previous chapters we discussed the theory supporting the use of process drama approaches in second language learning. We presented empirical findings when this approach was used in several L2 classrooms and considered the procedures for planning drama-oriented curricula to suit different needs and purposes. This chapter explores the links between theory, teaching, learning and assessment.

Many teachers feel that selecting or designing evaluation is one of the most difficult aspects of their practice. Any assessment procedure must match closely what has been taught. Because of the dynamic and unpredictable nature of drama activities, constructing meaningful assessments becomes an even more complicated and challenging task for language teachers.

A number of important issues must be considered when evaluating L2 learners' development in drama. First, when should evaluation take place? Do we document and assess what the students achieve in drama during the course, or evaluate the students at the end of the course in order to determine their progress? Are both types of evaluation informative? A second issue concerns the aspects of students' performance which are to be evaluated. Language teachers who favor the drama approach must decide why they have chosen to work in this way before they start the course: for example, to improve the learners' communicative ability, to establish links with the readings to be assigned to inspire writing topics. The type of evaluation they use should be selected according to the desired goals of their teaching. The third question is how do we evaluate students objectively? What assessment instruments will be appropriate for evaluating students during the course or at the end? How do we determine students' progress over time in a drama-oriented L2 language classroom? These questions will frame our discussion in this chapter.

Before we discuss these questions in detail, we want to clarify the features that produce a successful assessment. In 1985, the American Psychological Association, the American Education Research Association, and the National Council of Mathematics Educators agreed that *validity* is the most important consideration in test evaluation. Validity here refers to the appropriateness, meaningfulness and usefulness of the assessment developed for a particular group of learners or a particular course. If an assessment is not valid, it will not correctly reflect the outcomes of teaching and learning, and its results will have very little value to teachers and learners. Cases where students are evaluated with invalid instruments are not rare in our field. For example, we often find that students who learn a second language through the communicative approach are assessed with non-communicative tests. Instead of measuring the students communicative competence, the test either assesses the discrete points of their linguistic knowledge or are not conducted in a communicative manner.

In order to achieve validity, any assessment must be grounded in the theory of the teaching approach that is used. Where a drama approach has been implemented, the theory presented in Chapters Two and Five must be taken as the foundation of the assessment. Since the end-product of learning in a process-oriented L2 classroom is the experience the students have acquired during the activities, assessment methods must take this feature into account. This approach emphasizes the importance of communicating in authentic contexts; therefore assessment must take place in a natural and communicative setting.

For classroom teachers, the second key feature of a successful test is its *feasibility* in the school setting. In other words, an assessment which is valid for researchers may not be useful for school teachers unless it is easy to administer and score. Many assessment procedures used in research studies may not be directly applicable in the school environment because they are either too complicated or too time-consuming for teachers already occupied by their teaching schedules. However, after appropriate modification, these research-oriented testing methods can prove very valuable for classroom teachers. The feasibility of any evaluation form should be tested in classroom-based studies. In Chapter Three we presented several scoring systems for measuring L2 learners' communicative competence developed through drama activities. These scoring procedures can be used regularly in any classroom for similar purposes.

Keeping in mind the general principles for constructing valid and feasible assessments, this chapter focuses on strategies for developing appropriate evaluation methods for different types of drama-oriented classrooms.

CHARACTERISTICS OF VALID EVALUATION FOR DRAMA-ORIENTED L2 CLASSROOMS

Process drama approach is a recent development in the field of L2 learning and teaching. Documented research about the construction of valid testing procedures using this approach is particularly scarce. However, because this approach shares many features with those of Communicative Teaching and Learning Approach and Whole Language Approach, tests that reflect the underlying theories of those two well-established approaches are usually appropriate for measuring learners' L2 development in drama. For example, tests that integrate the four components of communicative competence—*grammatical, sociolinguistic, discourse,* and *strategic competence*—are especially useful for evaluating L2 learners in a drama-oriented course.

Appropriate measurements for an L2 course based on a process drama approach should

1. Evaluate the dynamic negotiation of meaning between participants within drama frames. This might include, for example, drama developed in class, texts used to initiate or structure the drama or readings assigned as homework.
2. Take place in meaningful and natural settings so as to elicit students' true competence in the target language and their understanding of the course material.
3. Be individualized and context specific to meet the particular goals of the course.
4. Include measures of both written and spoken language.
5. Evaluate not only students' end-of-course performance, but also monitor their development during the course, so as to provide an overall picture of the teaching/learning process.
6. Provide the teacher with the scores of the students' learning outcomes as well as allowing both students and teacher to evaluate the effectiveness of their work.

AVAILABLE INSTRUMENTS FOR EVALUATING L2 LEARNERS' VERBAL COMMUNICATION ABILITY DEVELOPED IN DRAMA

Since verbal interaction is at the center of drama activities, many L2 teachers favor this approach in order to improve L2 learners' communication ability. Tests designed to assess these aspects of L2 development are popular among language teachers and may include *oral presentation, different types of interviews, picture description, interaction tasks* and *role-play.* Tests of this kind are usually taken at the end of a semester or school year. Interaction is supposedly the key feature of all these tests. However, due to differences in format and administration procedures, the interaction levels of these tests vary enormously. Teachers must be aware of the different effects on scores when these tests are used. A brief review of some of the most popular tests is presented below.

Oral Presentation

The candidate is asked to give a short speech on a topic which has either been given to the candidate to prepare beforehand at home or shortly before the presentation in front of the examiner. This is an effective test format for gathering extensive speech data from candidates. Their linguistic knowledge of the target language and their ability to organize and present information can be judged from the data.

However, this kind of test has many disadvantages. First, if the candidates are familiar with the topic, they can memorize it. In this case, whatever is presented will not reveal the true oral ability of the candidate; consequently, test results will have very little value. Second, the presentation itself is neither interactive nor contextualized. Although the candidate faces the examiner when speaking, no conversation is carried on between them, so that the atmosphere in which the test takes place is likely to be both tense and unnatural. A modified version of this type of test occurs when the examiner asks the candidate a few questions based on the contents of the speech that has been presented. This post-presentation interview provides a degree of interaction, but it also has the disadvantages of the interview format. We discuss this point in detail in the next section.

Different Types of Interviews

The two most frequently used interview formats are the free interview and the controlled interview. Free interviews have no pre-set procedures or structures. They resemble an extended conversation between the interviewer and the candidate, who can interact freely as the interview progresses. The discourse patterns created in this test format are said to parallel normal patterns of social interaction in real life. As there are no pre-determined agendas and procedures, the conversation topics and discourse styles generated during the interviews vary from one candidate to another and will greatly influence the interviewer's judgment of the candidates' performance. In other words, there are no standardized criteria for evaluating candidates, and as a result of which, the credibility of the results is questionable.

Controlled interviews are considerably more popular than free interviews among language teachers. The basic difference between the free and the controlled interview is that the latter has pre-set procedures and/or topics. It is argued that these predetermined procedures have a higher degree of face and content validity than many other oral testing formats and can elicit comparable oral discourse from candidates during the interview. Standardized procedures also provide clear criteria for interviewers, who receive training beforehand and score the candidates during or after the interviews. Many widely used oral tests are constructed according to the theory of the controlled interview, such as the Ilyin Oral Interview (Ilyin, 1976), the Bilingual Syntax Measure (BSM) (Burt, Dulay, & Hernandez-Chavez, 1975) and FSI Oral Interview (see Adams & Fitt, 1979; Wilds, 1975).

These standardized oral interviews differ in their degree of structuring. The Ilyin Oral Interview and BSM, for example, are highly structured interview techniques, based on a sequence of pictures or a cartoon story with accompanying questions seeking to elicit certain grammatical structures from candidates. Both tests measure the discrete point of candidates' linguistic knowledge rather than their ability to communicate. FSI Oral Interview is a more open-ended test format in which one member of a well-trained two-person team interacts with the candidate on one topic and the other member observes and scores the performance based on the features of pronunciation, grammar, vocabulary, fluency, and comprehension (see UCLE/RSA Certificates in Communication Skills in English, in Weir, 1990 for detailed descriptions of this test).

Although controlled interviews achieve high validity and credibility in scoring, the first drawback of tests of this type is that they can neither cover the kinds of situations one may encounter in real life communication, nor can they replicate all the features of authentic conversation. The second disadvantage is that the participants are constrained by their roles as examiner and examinee. Since the examiner has tight control over the interaction, the dialogue generated during the test is very different from the everyday communication of two interlocutors of equal status.

Picture Description

This test format requires the candidate to tell a story or describe an event to the examiner based on a sequence of ordered pictures, or to answer a set of questions about the content of one particular picture chosen by the examiner. This technique is widely used in schools as it is easy to construct and administer. Because the instruction is clear and does not require the candidate to read or listen, this format is supposed to measure only the candidate's speaking ability. This is one of the few oral testing techniques that can elicit continuous speech from the candidates on the same topic or event. As a result, the discourse samples can be evaluated according to pre-determined criteria, for example the candidate's pronunciation, fluency, ability to use certain grammatical forms, and organize information. The value of the technique relies on the clarity of the pictures. Cultural and educational bias can be avoided when these pictures are carefully selected.

There are two problematic features in this technique. First, owing to its specific testing procedure, it elicits only one type of discourse, namely description. Second, it tells very little about the candidate's capacity for interaction, since there is no actual interlocutor to interact with. The first point may not always be a shortcoming because the test can elicit reliable data if the purpose of the evaluation is to assess the candidate's ability to describe events. In order to overcome the second problem, a modified version of this technique was suggested by Brown and Yule (1983). In this version, the candidate needs to describe the event according to the correct sequence of the pictures to a naive listener who thus needs to organize the orders of the pictures based on the description provided by the candidate. The listener is not allowed to ask questions. The entire process is tape-recorded and the candidate's speech is evaluated according to pre-determined criteria, for example, the clarity of the description.

The most important difference between the original and the modified versions of this test is that in the latter form the candidate is motivated to communicate information because the listener relies on what is said in order to arrange the pictures correctly. Although the listener is not allowed to respond verbally to the candidates, this aspect of the task is authentic communication. The data collected in this modified version of picture description is thus more authentic than those obtained in the original version. Because the examiner already knows the correct answers, in the original version of the test the candidate has no functional motivation or purpose for performing the task. In Chapter Three, in our study of how Chinese university students participated in drama activities, we adopted the modified version of the picture description technique in the pre- and post-oral tests. Please refer to Chapter Three for details of how actual data can be evaluated and quantified.

Interaction Tasks

This test is a kind of information-gap activity that many language teachers use in their classrooms. The test requires students to work either in pairs or with an examiner. Each participant is given only part of the information needed to complete the task. To fill in the gap, they need to get the missing information from each other through verbal communication. This testing technique elicits speech data in a truly interactive, purposeful, and contextualized situation. In order to obtain sufficient information to complete the task, participants have to use many linguistic forms, for example, asking and answering questions, clarifying and confirming information, paraphrasing, and so on. The richness and variety of language used in the task provides valuable information for evaluating the participants' communicative ability.

There are some points the teacher needs to consider before using this test. First, if the task is to be performed by two students and one of them has higher verbal ability than the other, the entire process may be dominated by the more able student and the less competent one will have little opportunity to demonstrate any potential in communication. If the task is to be completed by one student and the examiner, the examiner will be able to control his/her own level of participation so as to allow equal opportunity to the student to contribute to the communication process. However, because the examiner is familiar with the task, the test becomes less authentic. It is often more daunting for students to interact with examiners than with fellow students, and thus the presence of the examiner is likely to affect the candidate's performance during the test.

Role Play

In this type of test, the candidate is expected to play one of the roles in a situation which may occur in real life. The test can take place between two students or a student and the examiner. The results obtained from the use of this technique can achieve very high face and content validity, because the task itself generates a wide variety of situations that resemble everyday communication. The candidate's ability to participate effectively in interaction can be determined and evaluated accurately.

Like the information gap task, this technique has several drawbacks, whether it takes place between two students or a student and the examiner. Experience shows that extroverted students often take advantage of introverted students in this kind of task. Students who are familiar with the given situation also do better than those who are not, irrespective of their ability to interact. If the examiner takes one of the roles and participates in the interaction with the candidate, similar disadvantages to those described in the previous section will arise. Moreover, examiners will have great difficulty in evaluating the candidates' performance when they themselves are taking part in the interaction.

Discussion

The five types of oral testing techniques outlined above are all widely used by L2 language teachers for evaluating students' achievement on different occasions—on a national scale or after a particular course. It is difficult to conclude which one is better than the other, because each may be appropriate for a particular occasion or purpose. L2 language teachers and test designers, however, must share the following perspectives if they want to profit from using these tests.

First, it is inadvisable to score students at the moment the task is taking place. Bias can occur if the examiner tries to evaluate the candidates performance at the same time as administering the test. Paralinguistic features and dynamic communicative characteristics, for example, may be neglected if scoring takes place on the spot. Misjudgments are inevitable and, even worse, cannot be recovered if there is no reliable record of the test procedure. A more appropriate method is to document the entire test procedure with a tape-recorder or video camera and evaluate the candidates later. In this way the data can be scored by more than one evaluator, double checked and filed for future reference.

Second, we are interested in what students can do, but not what we want them to do in the drama. Educators should explore ways to assess what all students already know and can achieve.

Third, spoken data collected from these testing procedures may not all be easily quantifiable. Therefore, it is essential to develop a comprehensive marking system in order to avoid confusion in the evaluation.

Some may argue that there are practical difficulties in fulfilling the second and third requirements simultaneously. If too much freedom is given to the students during the testing procedure, it may be difficult to construct quantifiable marking schemes for scoring the data. Our suggestion is that one set of data collected from a test procedure should be approached from many different aspects, for example grammatical usage, correctness of pronunciation, social appropriateness, creativity, fluency in expression, and so on. As long as we clearly define the features within each aspect when scoring the data, we will obtain a general picture of what the students can do by synthesizing the results of different evaluation aspects.

PROCEDURES FOR ASSESSING STUDENTS' PERFORMANCE DURING THE COURSE

Traditionally, the assessment of what students have gained from instruction occurs at a few discrete points of time during the course, for example, during the mid-term and final evaluations. However, if we believe learning takes place over a period of time, it is necessary to pay attention to what students are doing in class throughout the course. Documenting students' performance in drama activities in the classroom and collecting students' course work allows teachers to look at what they can do from a completely different perspective. Data of this type will also provide valuable information about how teaching has been carried out, and will help teachers evaluate their own performance. In this section, two procedures are discussed: (1) documenting and evaluating classroom-based data both for understanding the students' and the teacher's performance and (2) portfolio assessment.

Evaluating Student and Teacher Performance From Classroom-Based Data

Observing the classroom has long been part of the task of L2 teachers. Many observe intuitively; some keep informal records of what has happened in their classes. However, these teachers also recognize the limitations of using databases, because knowledge about teaching and learning does not automatically emerge from the data, especially if the data are not properly documented. In addition, without appropriate and systematic interpretation of the data, classroom observation is merely a state-of-the-art survey that contributes little to our actual understanding of the profession (Candlin, in van Lier, 1988). Consequently, in order to understand the teaching and learning process, L2 teachers should first document classroom activities carefully and then analyze and interpret the data in a scientific manner. The results of the analysis should not be restricted to scoring students, but also used to diagnose the strengths and weaknesses of classroom teaching.

The process of analyzing classroom data is as follows:

Step One: Documenting Drama Activities
Video and audio recording is the optimal method of collecting data from a drama-oriented L2 classroom. Video recording can faithfully document the participants' physical movements in the space along with the facial expressions and sounds generated during the activities. However, due to the conditions in most classrooms, unless all the participants wear special wireless microphones for the recording, the clarity and volume of the sound are likely to be unstable. Unidentifiable audio records may cause serious problems when transcriptions are made later from the raw data. To solve this problem, we can hang several microphones at different places on the classroom ceiling to collect audio data when video-taping the activity. In this way, acoustically adequate and understandable data may be obtained along with the visual record. Field notes about the session should

be made by the teacher immediately after each class. These will provide additional information about the way in which the drama was initiated and maintained, and will detail any interruptions and interventions. An important condition of collecting useful video data is to do it regularly in the classroom. At first, students may feel uneasy about the presence of the video camera and audio recorder(s), but when recording has become routine in each session, students are likely to behave naturally in the drama.

Step Two: Transcribing the Data

After the raw data have been collected, a transcription should be prepared from the audio/video records. The transcriptions should be created so that the interactional situations can be easily reconstructed by the reader. There are transcription conventions developed by researchers in the field of discourse analysis and classroom studies. Transcribing data according to these conventions can help avoid the confusion of using different symbols or formats. Some widely recognized conventions have been suggested by van Lier (1988) (see Table 6.1 for the transcription conventions).

The transcription of data quoted in Chapters Three and Four are based on these conventions. If video-tapes are not available while reviewing the transcriptions, detailed notes about participants' physical movements must be specified along with their verbal utterances. Speech turns should also be indicated before each speaker's utterance to aid future analysis.

Step Three: Analyzing and Interpreting Data

The transcribed data can be used in many ways. The simplest approach is to *review* the video-tapes for diagnostic purposes with the students in class. The purpose is not primarily to compare or score the students. Instead, watching the tape with the students allows both teacher and students to reflect on how the drama was generated and transacted. Students should be encouraged to comment on their difficulties and on the strategies they used when interacting with their peers in the drama. Appropriate support and instruction can then be provided by the teacher. This is a valuable discussion and self-evaluation process for the learners.

Another way of using the data is to analyze some particular discourse area: for example, the students' pronunciation, vocabulary choices, communication strategies, participation levels, repair tactics or turn-taking. Once the teacher has developed an analytical system, the data can be analyzed accordingly. The evaluation process of the study of 33 Taiwanese students provides an example of the kind of information that may be obtained from this kind of discourse analysis. In that study, the students were evaluated on four initiative areas: topic management, self-selection, allocation, and sequencing (see Chapter Three). The same set of data can

TABLE 6.1.
Transcription Conventions

T	: teacher
S1, S2, etc.,	: identified student
XL	: unidentified learner
LL	: several or all participants simultaneously
/yes//yah//	: overlapping or simultaneous listening responses,
///okay///	brief comments, etc., by two, three, or an unspecified number of learners unspecified number of learners
=	: (1) turn continues below, at the next identical symbol or (2) if inserted at the end of one speaker's turn and the beginning of the next speaker's adjacent turn, it indicates that there is no gap at all between the two turns
. , .. , ... , etc.	: pause; three periods approximate one second. These periods are separated from the preceding word by a space.
?	: rising intonation, not necessarily a question
!	: a strong emphasis with falling intonation
okay. now. ,etc.	: a period unseparated from the preceding word indicates falling (final) intonation
so, and, etc.	: a comma indicates low-rising intonation, suggesting continuation
e:h, the:::, etc.	: one or more colons indicates lengthening of the preceding sound
really	: italic type indicates marked prominence through pitch or amplitude
okay? so, next [yes, but-	: onset and end of overlap or insertion of concurrent turn for convenience a space can be inserted in the turn above, but this does not indicate a pause unless marked by periods.
.....(radio)	: single brackets indicates unclear or probable item
((laughter)) ((unint))	: double brackets indicates (a stretch of) unintelligible sound (approximate length indicated), or comments about the transcript, including non-verbal actions
no-	: a hyphen indicates an abrupt cut-off, with level pitch
how about Julie?	: capitals are only used for proper names, not to indicate beginnings of sentences
[bambo]	: square brackets indicate phonetic transcription

Source: Modified from van Lier (1988).

also be used to evaluate the effectiveness of teaching and lesson construction or as material for teacher training.

Portfolio Assessment

Educators advocating "whole language" and humanistic approaches suggest creating portfolios for L2 students as an alternative to traditional assessments. A portfolio is normally a file that contains a student's formal or informal written work produced over time for a course. However, work in other formats such as audio/video-taped records of drama activities, presentations of group projects, and reading reports can also be included in the portfolio to demonstrate different aspects of the students' language achievement. For beginning L2 or bilingual learners, the portfolios may include works in both their first and target languages. In addition to the students' work, teachers' and parents' comments on the students' work, observation notes about their classroom performance, or lists of activities in which the students are involved outside the school can all be included in the file. Not only students but teachers, administrators, and parents are all involved in and benefit from the evaluation process.

Because portfolios contain work done as part of the regular curriculum, they do not—unlike traditional tests—require specially allotted time for administration. The work collected in a portfolio reveals what a student can achieve under natural and normal conditions during, and often outside class time. Since students are involved in the creation of their portfolios, they can monitor their own learning processes closely. They can engage in self-evaluation—a goal that is difficult to achieve when standardized tests are used. For L2 teachers, portfolios reveal students' growth over time, students interests and strengths in their first and target languages, and the effectiveness of the current curriculum. From the information provided in portfolios, L2 teachers can form or reform programs and curricula as well as evaluate their own performance in the classroom.

For a drama-oriented L2 course, portfolio assessment is valuable. This is especially true when drama is used for multiple purposes in language learning, such as improving students' communication skills as well as reading and writing abilities. A variety of students' work can be collected in the portfolio so that there is a balance when evaluating different aspects of their performance. For example, a video-tape of how a group of students create drama together in the classroom will provide information about the students' abilities as well as their difficulties in communication. The students' written reflections on the themes of the drama and reports on the assigned readings related to their class activities will allow the teacher to understand the level and progress of their reading and writing abilities.

Although portfolio assessment has only been introduced to the field of L2 education in recent years, experiences of using it successfully with bilingual students at the primary school level have been widely reported. For example, in many provinces of Canada, teachers and students have started collecting course work from the first year of primary school and reported considerable benefit from this approach for evaluation. Moreover, Barrs (1990) and Barrs and associates (1988) have documented cases in a successful project developed in England. Over five hundred elementary schools in London adopted an evaluation tool "The Primary Language Record" for evaluating student progress in the language arts in the 1989–

1990 school year. A particularly interesting part of this report documents how bilingual and language minority students in mainstream environments benefited from this evaluation tool in terms of their actual progress in language development.

Unfortunately, portfolio assessment has not earned sufficient attention and popularity among L2 educators in the secondary or higher school settings. The major reservation about using portfolios as an evaluation tool is the difficulty of quantifying the various sorts of student work included in portfolios. In some countries where highly competitive national achievement tests determine students' educational future, the flexibility that portfolio assessment allows becomes its major drawback. The belief that portfolio assessment does not evaluate student work objectively and thus cannot provide reliable scores is a serious misunderstanding. Any type of student work, for example, essays, projects, reports, audio/video-tapes, can be scored scientifically as long as a systematic scoring matrix is developed beforehand. For those teachers who must prepare their students for standardized tests, portfolio assessment can be used in parallel with standardized mid-term and final evaluations to help students see their progress from a different angle. What students have achieved during the course along with the results of the standardized tests should count towards their final grade.

In our study described in Chapter Three, where a group of Taiwanese college students learned English conversation through drama, portfolio assessment was the major evaluation tool for giving grades to the participants. Although the main objective of the course was to improve the learners' communication ability, a variety of course work, outside readings, and group projects were assigned to the students as follow-ups to classroom activities. At the beginning of the semester many students expressed their insecurity at the lack of a textbook for this course, but the reports and assignments collected in their portfolios became faithful records of what they had achieved in class. Learning English through drama was no longer an abstract concept. Many students reflected in their journals that they could gradually see progress and often reviewed what they had done in class from their portfolios. For those students who were less competent in spoken English, completing different types of course work allowed them to demonstrate their strengths in other aspects of language learning, including reading and writing.

SUMMARY

Developing meaningful and useful assessments is one of the key elements of a successful course. Assessments must reflect the teaching philosophy underlying the course and at the same time elicit valuable information about the learning outcomes for students and the effectiveness of the course. In this chapter we discussed the key features of valid and feasible assessments for drama-oriented L2 classrooms. We also reviewed a few popular, standardized, and classroom-based procedures for evaluating L2 learners' development in drama. We emphasized that it is necessary to evaluate L2 learners from different perspectives in order to obtain a more complete picture of the strengths and weaknesses of each student.

Appendix A

QUESTIONNAIRE

A. Personal Data:

Name: _____   Sex: _____

Student ID:_____   Major: _____

Birthday: ___/___/___   Birth place:_____

        M / D / Y

B. Previous Experience in Studying English:

1. I started learning English at the age of _____.
2. I graduated from _____ Junior High School. The English course of this school emphasized (1) listening (2) speaking (3) reading (4) writing (5) grammar. _____ (You can choose more than one answer.)
3. I graduated from _____ Senior High School. The English course of this school emphasized (1) listening (2) speaking (3) reading (4) writing (5) grammar. _____ (You can choose more than one answer.)
4. Except from the textbooks used in the high school, I (1) often (2) occasionally (3) never had any contact with English materials. _____
   *If your answer is (3), please skip the rest of the questions of this section and continue doing Sections C and D.
   a. The written materials in English (e.g., magazines and newspaper) I had read include _____.
   b. The audio materials in English (e.g., radio programs or music tapes) I had listened to include _____.
   c. The video materials in English (e.g., TV programs or movies) I had watched include _____.

d. Have you had any experience in using English for communication?
(1) Yes (2) No _____
*If your answer is YES, please briefly describe the situations, purposes, and results of your conversation: _____.

e. Have you traveled in English speaking countries?
(1) Yes (2) No ___.
*If your answer is YES, where did you go and for how long?

_____.

f. Have you lived in English speaking countries?
(1) Yes (2) No _____.
*If your answer is YES, where did you live and for how long?

_____

C. Self-Evaluation:

1. Among the four language skills (i.e., listening, speaking, reading, and writing), your strongest one is _____, and the weakest one is _____.
2. On a 1 to 6 scale where 1 means Very Poor and 6 means Excellent, how do you evaluate your four language skills?
listening _____ speaking _____ reading _____ writing _____
D. What are your goals and purposes of learning English in this course and why? Please explain._____.

Appendix B

The Students' Personal Data and Previous Experience in Studying English

Name	Dept.	EE Score	Starting Age	Years of Studying	Instructional Emph.		Visited ES Countries	Extra Contact	Self Evaluation			
					Junior H.	Senior H.			L	S	R	W
Fenny	Bioloby	47	12	6	RG	RWG	N	N	2	2	3	3
Mary	Biology	60	13	6	WG	RW	N	S	3	1	4	2
Collins	Architect.	63	10	8	R	R	N	S	4	4	4	3
Sunny	Math.	71	12	6	RG	RWG	N	S	3	2	4	3
Tomy	Earth S.	40	13	6	R	LSRWG	N	S	4	3	3	2
Robin	Earth S.	60	12	6	RG	RWG	N	S	2	4	5	3
Cyllia	Earth S.	66	11	6	RG	RWG	N	S	2	1	4	3
Nigel	Physic.	60	13	6	RG	RWG	N	O	2	4	4	3
Dick	Architect.	54	13	6	R	RG	N	S	1	2	2	3
Frans	Architect.	%	10	8	LSRWG	LSRWG	Y	O	3	4	4	5
Jordan	Math.	41	13	6	RG	RG	N	S	2	1	2	2
Clive	Earth S.	69	12	6	RG	R	N	N	3	3	4	3
Caro	Math.	50	14	6	RG	RWG	N	S	3	2	4	3
Frank	Chemist.	68	12	6	LSW	LSRWG	N	S	3	4.5	4.5	4.5
Jelly	Earth S.	50	12	6	SWG	RWG	N	N	-	-	-	-
Kevin	Chemist.	34	13	6	S	W	N	N	1	2	2	2
Jason	Earth S.	55	13	6	R	RG	N	S	1	2	2	2
Damin	Earth S.	50	13	6	R	LRWG	Y	S	3	2	2	3
Phil	Med. Tec.	54	14	6	RWG	SRWG	N	S	2	2	5	3
Tony	Earth S.	67	13	6	LS	LS	N	O	4	4	4	4

(continued from previous page)

Name	Dept.	EE Score	Starting Age	Years of Studying	Instructional Emph.		Visited ES Countries	Extra Contact	Self Evaluation			
					Junior H.	Senior H.			L	S	R	W
Chou	Math.	55	12	6	G	WG	N	S	2	2	4	3
Geoff	Chemist.	61	10	8	LR	LRW	N	S	4	2	4	3
Edwin	Earth S.	50	12	6	G	R	N	N	2	2	3	3
Martin	Earth S.	55	14	6	SR	LRW	N	N	-	-	-	-
Grace	Biology	50	13	6	RG	RWG	N	S	2	3	4	3
Max	Math.	48	12	6	R	RW	N	S	3	2	3	2
Jen	Earth S.	50	12	6	LRG	RWG	N	S	1	1	1	2
Jacky	Biology	47	13	6	RG	RG	N	S	1	2	2	2
C.S.	Math	62	9	9	RG	SRW	N	S	4	4	4	3
Jane	Earth S.	#	12	6	WG	RWG	Y	S	3	4	4	4
Henry	Math.	30	13	6	SW	SWG	N	S	2	2	3	2
George	Earth S.	45	13	6	SRWG	LSRWG	N	S	2	2	1	1
		$X = 54.42$	$X = 12.17$	$X = 6.27$								

Notes: %: Overseas Chinese, didn't attend EE
#: Gifted student, didn't attend EE
EE: Entrance Exam

L: Listening   Total L = 6   Total L = 8
S: Speaking   S = 8   S = 8
R: Reading   R = 24   R = 29
W: Writing   W = 8   W = 25
G: Grammar   G = 21   G = 23

N: Never   S: Sometimes   Rank from 1 to 6
Y: Yes   O: Often   1: Lowest
                            6: Highest
                            @: didn't answer

N = 6   XL = 2.52
S = 24   XS = 2.53
O = 2   XR = 3.34
           XW = 2.82

Notes

[1]JCEE English test is a paper-and-pencil test with a full score of 100. It is designed to evaluate high school students' knowledge of English vocabulary, usage, sentence structure, and reading and writing skills by cloze, multiple-choice questions, reading comprehension questions, translations, and a shorts guided writing session.

[2]All students' journals were written in their native language—Chinese. The segments quoted in the following sections are our translation.

[3]S1, S2, and S3 were all learners. SS were unidentified learners. T was the researcher. Ab was a native speaker of English and also one of the two regular teachers of the class (American Teacher B).

List of Abbreviations

AERA	American Education Research Association
APA	American Psychological Association
BSM	Bilingual Syntax Measure
CLL	Community Language Learning
CU	communication unit
EFL	English as a foreign language
ESL	English as a second language
I-R-F pattern	Initiation-Response-Feedback pattern
JCEE	Joint Colleges Entrance Examination
L1	first language
L2	second language
NCME	National Council of Mathematics Education
PI	participation index
PL	participation level
PV	participation value
SI	Strategic Interaction
SLA	second language acquisition

References

Adams, M., & Frith, J. (Eds.). (1979). *Testing kit: French and Spanish.* Washington, DC: Foreign Service Institute.

Al-Khanji, R. (1987, April). *Strategic interaction: A method that enhances communicative competence.* Paper presented at the Annual Meeting of the International Association of Teachers of English as a Foreign Language, Westencle, Belgium.

Allwright, D. (1988). *Observation in the language classroom.* London: Longman.

Altwerger, B., Edelsky, C., & Flores, B. M. (1987). Whole language: What's new. *The Reading Teacher, 41,* 144–154.

American Psychological Association. (1985). *Standards for educational and psychological testing.* Washington, DC: American Psychological Association.

Anderson, M. L. (1989). *Theatre techniques for language learning: Assumptions and suggested progression activities.* (ERIC Document Reproduction Service No. ED 321 572).

Austin, J. L. (1962). *How to do things with words.* Oxford: Clarendon Press.

Bahktin, M. M. (1986). *Speech genres and other late essays* (p. 75). Austin, TX: The University of Texas Press.

Barrs, M. (1990). The primary language record: Reflection of issues in valuation. *Language Arts, 67*(3), 244–253.

Barrs, M., Ellis, S., Hester, H., & Thomas, A. (1988). *The primary language record: Handbook for teachers.* Portsmouth, NH: Heinemann.

Bellack, A. A., Kliebard, M. M., Hyman, R. T., & Smith, F. L. (1966). *The language of the classroom.* New York: Teachers' College Press.

Bernhardt, E. B. (Ed.) (1992). *Life in language immersion classrooms.* Clevedon, Avon: Multilingual Matters.

Booth, D. (1994). *Story drama: Reading, writing and roleplaying across the curriculum.* Markham: Pembroke Publishers.

Brown, G., & Yule, G. (1983). *Teaching the spoken language: An approach based on the analysis of conversational English.* Cambridge: Cambridge University Press.

Brumfit, C. (1980). *From defining to designing: Communicative specifications versus communicative methodology in foreign language teaching.* Mimeograph, University of London Institute of Education.

Brumfit, C. (1982). Some humanistic doubts about humanistic language teaching. In C. Brumfit (Ed.), *Humanistic approaches: An empirical view.* London: British Council. (ERIC Document Reproduction Service No. ED 258 464).

Bruner, J. (1986). *Actual minds, possible worlds.* Cambridge, MA: Harvard University Press.

Burt, M., Dulay, H., & Hernandez-Charez, E. (1975). *Bilingual syntax measure.* New York: Harcourt Brace Jovanovich.

Byron, K. (1986). *Drama in the English classroom.* London: Methuen.

Courtney, R. (1992). *Drama and intelligence.* Montreal: McGill Queen's University Press.

Coyle, J. M., & Bisgyer, D. M. (1984). *What constitutes "genuine" communication in the adult L2 classroom? A search for a definition through classroom observation research.* Washington DC: Washington Consulting Group, Inc.

Curran, C. (1976). *Counseling learning in second languages.* Apple River, IL: Apple River Press.

Deckert, C. D. (1987). *The Communicative approach: Helping students adjust.* In Forum Vol. XXV No. 3, Washington, DC: Government Printing Office.

Dinsmore, D. (1985). Waiting for Godot in the EFL Classroom. *English Language Teaching Journal, 39,* (4), 225–234.

Di Pietro, R. J. (1982a). *The concept of personal involvement in foreign language study.* Originally presented at the Modern Language Association Annual Meeting Los Angeles, CA. (ERIC Document Reproduction Service No. ED227684).

Di Pietro, R. J. (1982b). The open-ended scenario: A new approach to conversation. *TESOL Quarterly, 16,* 15–20.

Di Pietro, R. J. (1983, December). *The element of drama in strategic interaction.* Paper presented at the Centennial Convention of the MLA. (ERIC Document Reproduction Service No. ED 238 284).

Di Pietro, R. J. (1985). *Roles in the foreign language classroom.* Paper resented at the Seventh Delaware Symposium of Language Studies.

Di Pietro, R. J. (1986, March). *Scenario discourse: Its contribution to L2 acquisition.* Paper presented at the Annual Meeting of the Teachers of English to speakers of other languages, Anaheim, CA.

Di Pietro, R. J. (1987a). *Strategic interaction: Learning languages through scenarios.* Cambridge: Cambridge University Press.

Di Pietro, R. J. (1987b, August). *Interactive discourse in the L2 classroom.* Paper resented at AILA Conference, University of Sydney, Australia.

Edmiston, B. W. (1991). *"Where have you travelled?": A teacher-researcher study of structuring drama for reflection and learning.* Unpublished doctoral dissertation, The Ohio State University, Columbus, Ohio.

Edmondson, W. J. (1985). Discourse worlds in the classroom and in the foreign language learning. *Studies in Second Language Acquisition, 7,* (2): 159–168.

Ellis, R. (1984). *Classroom second language development.* Oxford: Pergamon Press.

Ellis, R. (1986). *Understanding second language acquisition.* Oxford: Oxford University Press.

Ellis, R. (Ed.). (1987). *Second language acquisition in context.* Englewood Cliffs, NJ: Prentice Hall.

Ellis, R. (1988). *Classroom second language development.* Hemel Hempstead, Hertfordshire: Prentice Hall

Ellis, R. (1990). *Instructed second language acquisition.* Cambridge, MA: Blackwell.

Freeman, Y. S., & Freeman, D. E. (1992). *Whole language for second language learners.* Portsmouth, NH: Heinemann.

Friere, P. (1972). *Pedagogy of the oppressed.* Harmondsworth, Middlesex: Penguin.

Gattegno, C. (1972). *Teaching foreign languages in schools: The silent way.* New York: Educational Solutions.

Gattegno, C. (1976). *The common sense of teaching foreign languages.* New York: Educational Solutions.

Green, J. L., & Harker, J. O. (1988). *Multiple perspective analysis of classroom discourse.* Norwood, NJ: Ablex.

Gremmo, M., Holec, H., & Riley, P. (1978). Taking the initiative: Some pedagogical applications of discourse analysis. *Melanges Pedagogique,* University of Nancy: CHAPEL.

Holden, S. (1981). *Drama in language teaching.* London: Longman.

Holmes, J. (1978). *Sociolinguistic competence in the classroom.* In J. Richards (Ed.). Understanding Second and Foreign Language Learning. Rowley, Mass.: Newbury House.

Ilyin, D. (1976). *Ilyin oral interview.* Powley, MA: Newbury House.

Johnson, D. M. (1988). ESL children as teachers: A social view of second language use. *Language Arts, 65,* (2), 156.

Johnson, L., & O'Neill, C. (Eds.). (1984). *Dorothy Heathcote: Collected writings on education and drama.* Evanston, IL: Northwestern University Press.

Jones, R.L., & Spolsky, B. (Eds.). (1985). *Testing language proficiency.* Burlington, VA: Center for Applied Linguistics.

Kao, S. M. (1992). *A case study of second language learners' participation in a drama-oriented conversation class.* Paper granted by National Science Council, R.O.C.

Kao, S. M. (1994). *Classroom interaction in a drama-oriented English conversation class of first-year college students in Taiwan: A teacher-researcher study.* Unpublished doctoral dissertation, The Ohio-State University. Paper granted by National Science Council, R.O.C.

Kao, S. M. (1995). From script to impromptu: Learning a second language through process drama. In P. Taylor & C. Hoepper (Eds.), *Selected readings in drama and theatre education: The IDEA'95 papers,* (pp. 88–101). Brisbane, Australia: National Association for Drama in Education Publications.

Kapser, G. (1979). Communication strategies: Modality reduction. *Interlanguage Studies Bulletin, 4,* (2), 266–283.

Khanji, R. (1987). *Strategic interaction: A method that enhances communicative competence.* (ERIC Document Reproduction Service No. ED 287 301).

Kramsch, C. J. (1985). Classroom interation and discourse options. *Studies in Second Language Acquisition, 7*(2): 169–183.

Krashen, S. (1985). *The input hypothesis: Issues and implications.* New York: Longman.

Lantolf, J., & Khanji, R. (Eds.). (1982). *Nonlinguistic factors in L2 performance: Expanding the L2 research paradigm.* Paper presented at the Ninth LACUS Forum, Northwestern University.

Le français à l'élémentaire: Programme d'études. (1987). Edmonston: Alberta Education.

Lozanov, G. (1979). *Suggestology and outlines of suggestopedy.* New York: Gordon and Breach.

Maley, A., & Duff, A. (1978). *Drama techniques in language learning.* Cambridge: Cambridge University Press, reprinted in 1995.

Maley, A., & Duff, A. (1991). *Drama techniques in language teaching: A resource book of communication activities for language teachers* (2nd ed.). Cambridge: Cambridge University Press.

McGregor, L., Tate, M., & Robinson, K. (1977). *Learning through drama.* London: Heinemann.

Miller, M. L. (1986, November). *Using drama to teach foreign languages.* Paper presented at the Annual Meeting of the Japan Association of Language Teachers International Conference on Language Teaching and Learning.

Moreno, J. L. (1959). *Psychodrama: Volume II: Foundations of psychotherapy.* Beacon, NJ: Beacon House.

Morgan, N., & Saxton, J. (Eds.). (1987). *Teaching drama: A mind of many wonders.* London: Hutchinson.

Nunan, D. (1987). Communicative language teaching: Making it work. *English Language Teaching Journal, 4,* (2), 136–145.

O'Neill, C. (1992). *Building dramatic worlds in process. Reflections: A booklet of shared ideas on process drama.* Columbus, OH: Ohio Drama Education Exchange.

O'Neill, C. (1995). *Drama worlds: A framework for process drama.* Portsmouth, NH: Heinemann.

O'Neill, C., & Lambert, A. (Eds.). (1982). *Drama structures.* London: Hutchinson.

O'Neill, C., Lambert, A., Linnell, R., & Warr-Wood, J. (1976). *Drama guidelines.* London: Longman.

Radin, B. (1985). *Dramatic techniques in ESL instruction.* (ERIC Document Reproduction Service No. ED 256 174).

Rardin, P. R., Tranel, D. D., Tirone, P. L., & Green, B. D. (1988). *Education in a new dimension: The counseling–learning approach to community language learning.* Chicago: Counseling-Learning Publication.

Rogers, C. (1975). The interpersonal relationship in the facilitation of learning. In D. Read & S. Simon, (Eds.), *Humanistic education sourcebook.* Englewood Cliffs, NJ: Prentice Hall.

Rudduck, J., & Hopkins, D. (1985). *Research as a basis for teaching: Readings from the work of Lawrence Stenhouse.* London: Heinemann Educational Books.

Savignon, S. (1983). *Communicative competence: Theory and classroom practice.* Reading, MA: Addison-Wesley.

Sendak, M. (1963). *Where the wild things are.* Harper Trophy.

Shacker, D. L., Juliebo, M. F., & Parker, D. (1993). Using drama in the foreign immersion program. *Youth Theater Journal, 8,* (1), 3–10.

Shor, I., & Friere, P. (Eds.). (1987). *A Pedagogy for liberation: Dialogues on transforming education.* South Hadley, MA: Bergin and Garvey.

Sinclair, J., & Coulthard, R. (1975). *Towards an analysis of discourse.* London: Oxford University Press.

Sjørslev, S. (1987, June). *Some aspects of classroom interaction. Equality in language learning:* Proceedings of the Nordic Conference of Applied Linguistics (5th Jyvaskyla, Finland). AFiaLA series, No. 5, 188–196.

Smith, S. M. (1984). *The theater arts and the teaching of second languages*. Reading, MA: Addison-Wesley.

Snyman, A., & De Kock, D. M. (Eds.). (1991). Problem solving and creative thinking in structured second language teaching. *The Journal of Creative Behaviour, 25*(3), 228–240.

Spoelders, M. (1987, June). *Verbal communication in the classroom. Equality in language learning:* Proceedings of the Nordic Conference of Applied Linguistics (5th Jyvaskyla, Finland). AFiaLA series, No. 5, 197–206.

Spolin, V. (1963). *Improvisation for the theater.* Evanston, IL: Northwestern University Press.

Stern, S. (1981). Drama in second language learning from a psycholinguistic perspective. *Language Learning, 30,* (1), 77–97.

Stevick, E. W. (1976). *Memory, meaning and method.* Rowley, MA: Newbury House.

Stevick, E. W. (1980). *Teaching languages: A way and ways.* Rowley, MA: Newbury House.

Stevick, E. W. (1982). *Humanism in humanistic approaches: An empirical view.* (ELT Document 113). British Council. (ERIC Document Reproduction Service No. ED 258 464).

Swartz, L. (1988). *Dramathemes: A practical guide for teaching drama.* Portsmouth, NH: Heinemann.

Tannen, D. (1989). *Talking voices.* Cambridge: Cambridge University Press.

Tarlington, C., & Verriour, P. (1991). *Role drama.* Portsmouth, NH: Heinemann.

van Lier, L. (1984a). Discourse analysis and classroom research: A methodological perspective. *International Journal of the Sociology of Language, 49,* 111–133.

van Lier, L. (1984b). Analysing interaction in second language classrooms. *English Language Teaching Journal, 38,* (3), 160–170.

van Lier, L. (1988). *The classroom and the language learner: Ethnography and second-language classroom research.* New York: Longman.

Via, R. (1987). "The magic if" of theater: Enhancing language learning through drama. In W. Rivers (Ed.), *Interactive language teaching.* New York: Cambridge University Press.

Vygotsky, L. (1978). *Mind in society.* Cambridge, MA: Harvard University Press.

Wagner, B. J. (1988). Research currents: Does classroom drama affect the arts of language? *Language Arts, 65*(1).

Weir, C. J. (1990). *Communicative language testing.* London: Prentice Hall.

Widdowson, H. G. (1978). *Teaching languages as communication.* Oxford: Oxford University Press.

Widdowson, H. G. (1990). *Aspects of language teaching.* Oxford: Oxford University Press.

Wiesner, D. (1991). *Tuesday.* New York: Clarion Books.

Wilburn, D. (1992). Learning through drama in the immersion classroom. In E. B. Bernhardt (Ed.), *Life in immersion classrooms.* Philadelphia, PA: Multilingual Matters.

Wilds, C. P. (1975). The oral interview test. In R. L. Jones & B. Spolsky (Eds.), *Testing language proficiency.* Arlington, VA: Center for Applied Linguistics.

Wright, A., Betteridge, D., & Buckby, M. (1980). *Games for language learning.* Cambridge: Cambridge University Press.

Author Index

Subject Index

Lightning Source UK Ltd.
Milton Keynes UK
UKOW06f1129051215

263953UK00027BA/440/P

9 781567 503692